ETSY SEO SECRETS

UNLOCK THE #1 RANK ON ETSY SEARCH RESULTS

By
Halcyon Press

Published by Halcyon Press

CONTENTS

Chapter 1:
The Etsy SEO Foundation

Understanding Etsy's search algorithm

Today, we're diving into the fascinating world of Etsy's search algorithm to help you understand how it functions. Trust me, it's not as complex as it might seem!

So, let's start by uncovering the secrets of this algorithm. Etsy's search algorithm aims to help buyers find the most relevant and engaging products. It considers various factors to determine search rankings, and understanding these can give you a competitive edge.

A key factor influencing search rankings on Etsy is relevance. The algorithm analyses your listing's title, tags, and description to assess its relevance to a buyer's search query. Thus, optimising these elements with relevant keywords and phrases is crucial. For instance, if you're selling handmade soap, include keywords like 'handmade soap', 'organic soap', or specific attributes that make your product unique.

One of the key factors that infuence search rankings on Etsy is relevance.

However, relevance isn't the only crucial factor. Customer experience also plays a significant role. Etsy aims to ensure a positive platform experience, rewarding sellers who provide exceptional service and satisfaction.

Why does customer experience matter for search rankings? When buyers enjoy a great experience with your shop, they're likelier to leave positive reviews, recommend you, and engage with your listings. All these actions boost your shop's reputation and, in turn, your search rankings.

To enhance customer experience, focus on offering excellent communication, prompt shipping, and superior packaging. Respond quickly to inquiries, provide detailed product descriptions, and ship orders promptly.

Moreover, Etsy considers customer reviews in determining search rankings. More positive reviews improve your chances of ranking higher. Satisfied customers are more likely to leave favourable reviews, so aim to provide top-quality products and service.

As an Etsy seller, your goal should be to optimise your listings for relevance and provide an exceptional customer experience. This approach will improve your search rankings and attract more buyers to your shop.

Remember, combining relevance with customer experience is key to success on Etsy. Put your best foot forward, delight your customers, and watch your search rankings climb!

Happy selling!

Keyword relevance and its importance

Understanding keyword relevance is vital for optimising your listings and improving search rankings. Keywords are the words or phrases customers use to search for products on Etsy. Incorporating relevant keywords increases your visibility and attracts potential buyers.

Keyword relevance means how closely your chosen keywords match potential customers' search terms. For instance, if you sell handmade jewellery, using keywords like 'unique earrings' and 'handcrafted necklaces' makes your listings more relevant to those specific searches.

Keyword relevance is crucial because Etsy's search algorithm looks for listings that are both relevant and high-quality. Relevant keywords boost your chances of appearing in search results.

Additionally, keyword relevance helps you stand out. Choosing accurate keywords targets specific customer needs and preferences. For example, if you sell unique vintage clothing, using keywords like 'retro dresses' or 'vintage fashion' attracts customers looking specifically for those items.

Let's delve into specific examples to illustrate the difference between relevant and non-relevant keywords for various products:

Handmade Jewellery:

Relevant Keywords:
'handcrafted silver necklace', 'amethyst pendant jewellery', 'artisan-crafted earrings'.

Non-Relevant Keywords:
'cheap fashion jewellery', 'factory-made accessories', 'mass-produced necklaces'.

Unique Vintage Clothing:

Relevant Keywords:
'vintage 1950s dresses', 'retro clothing', 'antique women's fashion'.

Non-Relevant Keywords:
'modern fashion dresses', 'contemporary women's wear', 'latest fashion trends'.

Handmade Soaps:

Relevant Keywords:
'organic lavender soap', 'handmade vegan soap', 'natural skincare products'.

Non-Relevant Keywords:
'commercial soap brands', 'chemical body wash', 'synthetic fragrances'.

Custom Artwork:

Relevant Keywords:
'custom portrait painting', 'hand-painted wall art', 'personalized canvas art'.

Non-Relevant Keywords:
'mass-produced prints', 'digital image downloads', 'stock photos'.

Eco-friendly Home Decor:

Relevant Keywords:
'sustainable home furnishings', 'recycled wood decor', 'eco-friendly living room accessories'.

Non-Relevant Keywords:
'plastic home decorations', 'artificial plants', 'non-biodegradable materials'.

Keyword relevance implies how closely your chosen keywords align with potential customers' search terms. For example, if you sell handmade jewellery, using specific keywords like 'unique silver earrings' or 'handcrafted gemstone necklaces' targets customers searching for those items directly.

Etsy's search algorithm prioritizes listings that are both relevant and high-quality. Accurate, relevant keywords enhance your visibility in search results and help you stand out by targeting specific customer interests and preferences. For instance, for unique vintage clothing, keywords like 'vintage flapper dresses' or 'classic retro fashion' will attract customers who are specifically searching these styles.

By choosing relevant keywords, you cater to the specific needs and preferences of your target audience. This targeted approach not only improves your visibility in search results but also helps in attracting the right kind of customer – those who are genuinely interested in what you have to offer.

Conversely, using non-relevant keywords can dilute your listing's effectiveness. For example, using broad or generic terms like 'clothes' or 'accessories' for vintage clothing might attract a wide range of shoppers, but many may not be interested in vintage styles specifically. This can lead to lower conversion rates and potentially affect your shop's reputation due to mismatched customer expectations.

In summary, the relevance of keywords in your Etsy listings is a critical factor in search optimization. It helps in aligning your products with the specific searches and needs of your target audience, thereby enhancing the chances of your listings being found and purchased. This strategic approach to keyword selection is key to standing out in a competitive marketplace like Etsy.

CUSTOMER SATISFACTION MATTERS
Providing a great customer experience is key to selling on Etsy.

Customer experience matters because positive interactions lead to increased sales, customer satisfaction, and higher search rankings.

The role of customer & marketplace experience

Providing a great customer and marketplace experience is key to selling on Etsy. It ensures customer satisfaction and boosts your search rankings. Here, we'll explore how a positive customer and marketplace experience impacts your Etsy SEO.

Customer experience matters because positive interactions lead to increased sales, customer satisfaction, and higher search rankings. Etsy prioritises shops with a good track record of exceptional service and a seamless marketplace experience. Consistently great customer experiences increase your visibility to potential buyers.

Enhancing your marketplace experience can boost your search rankings. Here are some tips:

1. Provide clear and detailed product descriptions:

Write clear and detailed product descriptions, including materials, dimensions, and customization options. This helps customers make informed decisions and improves visibility.

2. Offer excellent customer support:

Offer excellent customer support. Respond promptly and professionally to resolve issues, enhancing buyer confidence.

3. Optimize your shop policies:

Clearly outline shop policies on shipping, returns, and refunds. Transparency builds trust and credibility.

4. Consider offering free shipping or discounts:

Consider offering free shipping or discounts to attract customers and generate sales, benefiting both customers and your search ranking.

5. Pay attention to packaging and shipping

Focus on packaging and shipping. Well-packaged items and timely shipping enhance customer experience, leading to positive reviews and recommendations.

By focusing on customer and marketplace experience, you can improve your Etsy search rankings and attract more potential buyers. Providing a professional and enjoyable shopping experience benefits both your business and your customers.

Chapter 2:
Keyword Research Essentials

How to identify high-potential keywords

Effective keyword research is vital for giving your Etsy listings a competitive edge. This section will share some practical techniques and tools to help you identify high-potential keywords.

First, understand your target audience and their search intent. Think from your customers' perspective about what keywords they might use to find products like yours. Consider specific features, materials, or themes of your items. For instance, if you sell handmade earrings, suitable keywords could be 'boho earrings', 'dainty earrings', or 'statement earrings'.

Put yourself in the shoes of your customers and think about what keywords they might use to find products like yours.

Researching your competitors is another method to uncover high-potential keywords. Observe popular shops within your niche and note the keywords they use in their listings. This gives you insights into effective keywords but ensures you add a unique twist to distinguish your products.

Utilise keyword research tools like Google Keyword Planner, SEMrush, or Moz Keyword Explorer. They provide valuable data on search volume, competition, and related keywords, helping you find keywords with high search potential and lower competition.

Long-Tail Keywords vs Shorter Keywords:

Shorter Keywords: These are often broad and generic, leading to high competition. For example, 'earrings', 'soaps', or 'scarves'.

Long-Tail Keywords: These are more specific and targeted, usually resulting in lower competition and higher conversion rates. For example:

For handmade earrings: Instead of just 'earrings', use 'handmade crystal drop earrings' or 'vintage-inspired pearl stud earrings'.

For artisan soaps: Rather than 'soaps', use 'organic lavender shea butter soaps' or 'handcrafted charcoal exfoliating bars'.

For custom scarves: Instead of 'scarves', use 'handwoven wool winter scarves' or 'custom silk floral print scarves'.

The use of long-tail keywords such as 'handmade crystal earrings' or 'geometric brass earrings' can attract highly targeted customers who are searching for those specific types of products.

Regularly experiment with different keywords and monitor your Etsy shop's analytics to identify which keywords drive the most traffic and conversions. Continuously refine and optimise your keyword strategy based on these insights.

In conclusion, effective keyword research is a blend of understanding your audience, researching competitors, utilising keyword research tools, focusing on long-tail keywords, and engaging in continuous experimentation and refinement. This approach helps in pinpointing high-potential keywords that can significantly improve the visibility and success of your Etsy listings.

Tools for effective keyword research

When it comes to conducting effective keyword research on Etsy, there are several tools available that can help you discover valuable keywords and boost your listings' visibility. In this section, we will explore some of the popular keyword research tools that Etsy sellers can utilize to gain an edge in the competitive marketplace.

1. Etsy's Search Bar:

Etsy's own search bar is a great starting point for keyword research. Simply type in relevant search terms related to your products and see what other keywords Etsy suggests. This can give you insights into popular keywords that shoppers are using and help you optimize your listings accordingly.

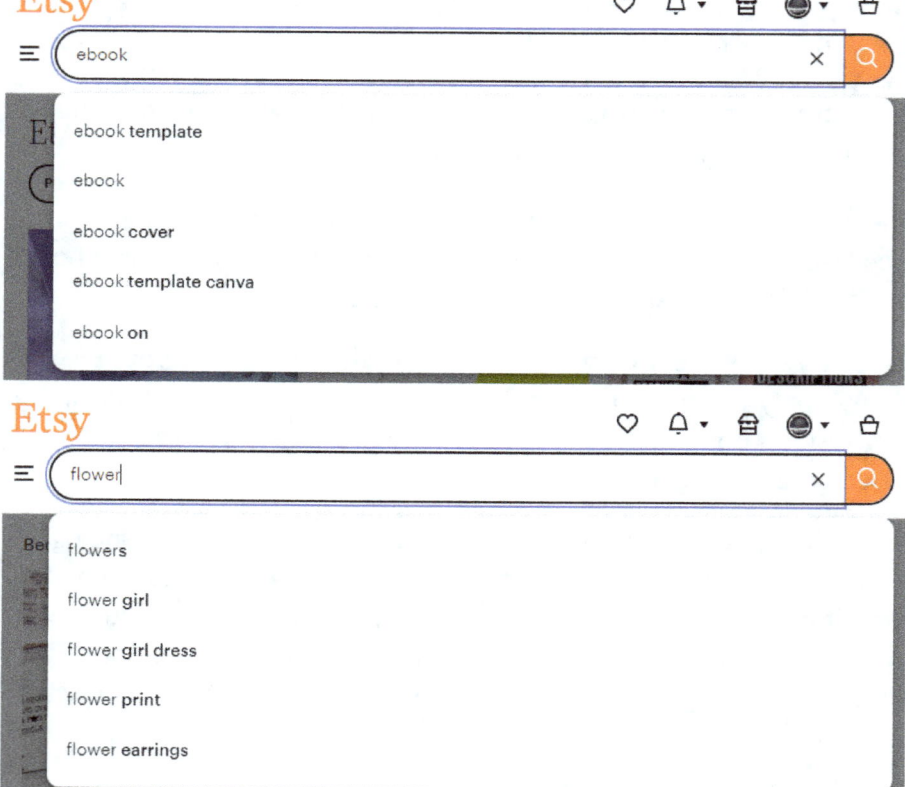

2. Google Keyword Planner:

Google Keyword Planner is another powerful tool that can be used for keyword research on Etsy. Although primarily designed for Google AdWords, it can also provide valuable keyword suggestions and estimate search volumes for specific terms. By understanding the search volume of certain keywords, you can target the ones with higher search volumes to reach a wider audience.

These tools are just the beginning. Utilize their features for insights that can significantly improve your Etsy listings' visibility.

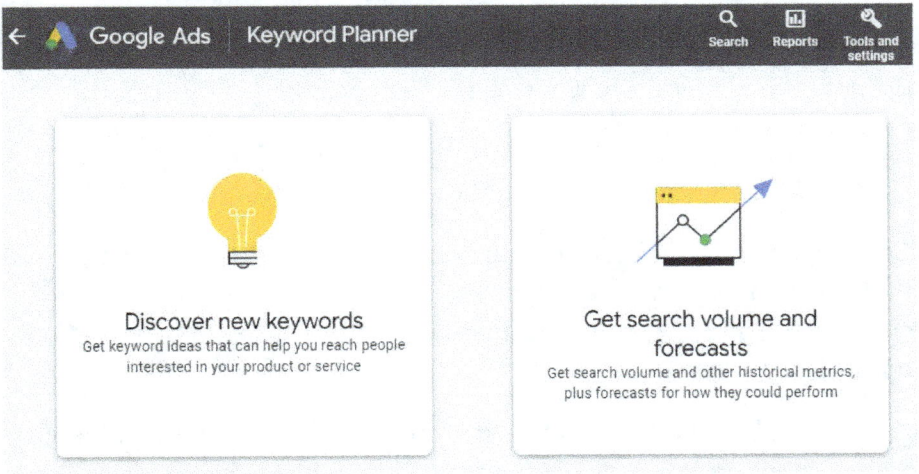

Analyzing competition and market demand

Choosing the right keywords is crucial for success on Etsy. Selecting less competitive keywords increases the likelihood of your products being seen and purchased. This section explores strategies to assess keyword competition and make informed choices.

To evaluate keyword competition, analyse the number of listings for a specific keyword search. A high number of listings indicates intense competition, whereas fewer listings suggest lower competition.

Also, assess the quality of top-ranking listings. Professionally presented listings with numerous positive reviews imply strong competition.

Research market demand for keywords using tools that provide search volume data and trends. This helps identify high-demand keywords.

Combine analyses of keyword competition and market demand to find keywords with a good balance. For instance, a keyword with low competition and high market demand presents a valuable optimisation opportunity.

Remember, finding effective keywords on Etsy requires continuous monitoring and adjustment based on evolving competition and market demand. Regular analysis helps you stay ahead and maximises your success chances.

Chapter 3: Crafting Perfect Listings

Optimising Titles for Relevancy and Click-Through

Optimising titles on Etsy is a critical step for attracting potential buyers and enhancing the visibility of your listings. It involves a delicate balance of professionalism and creativity to effectively engage your target audience.

Start by conducting comprehensive keyword research to understand the search phrases used by your potential customers. Including these keywords in your titles can significantly boost your chances of appearing in search results. For instance, if you're selling handmade soaps, incorporate specific keywords such as 'natural soap', 'artisan soap', or 'organic soap' in your titles. This strategy is more likely to attract buyers actively searching for these types of products.

Beyond just keyword inclusion, crafting titles that capture attention and encourage clicks

One of the key factors that infuence search rankings on Etsy is relevance.

is crucial. Here are some techniques and examples of titles that can achieve this:

Creating a Sense of Urgency or Exclusivity:

"Limited Edition Handcrafted Silk Scarves – Only 50 Available!"
"Exclusive Organic Soap Range – Get Yours Before They're Gone!"

Using Emotive Power Words:

"Stunning Hand-Painted Ceramic Vases – Brighten Up Your Home!"
"Luxurious Hand-Woven Woolen Blankets – Cozy Up in Style!"

Highlighting Unique Features:

"One-of-a-Kind Handmade Jewellery – Uniquely Yours!"
"Bespoke Wooden Furniture – Tailored to Your Taste!"

Creating Curiosity and Excitement:

"Discover the Magic of Our Aromatic Candle Collection!"
"Transform Your Space with Our Must-Have Vintage Mirrors!"

Combining Emotive Words with Specific Benefits:

"Indulge in Sumptuous Handmade Chocolates – A Taste Sensation!"
"Experience Ultimate Comfort with Our Soft Egyptian Cotton Towels!"

Remember to keep your titles concise, clear, and free from overly complex language. Regularly testing and refining your titles based on performance metrics is key to understanding what resonates best with your audience.

By continuously optimizing your titles with relevant keywords, urgency, exclusivity, and emotive power words, you can significantly improve the effectiveness of your titles in attracting clicks. This leads to enhanced SEO for your Etsy listings, ultimately contributing to greater visibility and success.

Creating Compelling Product Descriptions

As an Etsy Seller, mastering the art of compelling product descriptions is key to converting browsers into buyers. This subchapter delves into the strategies for crafting descriptions that not only inform but also entice your audience.

Understand Your Audience:

Know who you're selling to. Tailor your descriptions to address their specific needs and queries.

Highlight Benefits:

Focus on how your product improves the customer's life. For instance, describe how a handmade leather bag's spacious compartments and durable material offer both style and functionality.

Use Persuasive Language:

Employ phrases that create urgency or desire, like 'Get yours now' or 'Limited stock available', to spur potential customers into action.

Weave a Story:

Narratives engage emotionally. Share the inspiration or craftsmanship behind your product to connect with your audience on a deeper level.

Incorporate Social Proof:

Use customer testimonials or reviews to build trust and credibility, reassuring potential buyers of their purchase decision.

Concise and Scannable:

In our fast-paced world, brevity is key. Use bullet points or short paragraphs to break up text and highlight important information.

3: CRAFTING PERFECT LISTINGS

UNDERSTAND YOUR AUDIENCE
Be crystal clear on who you're selling to, their needs and queries.

As an Etsy Seller, mastering the art of compelling product descriptions is key to converting browsers into buyers.

Add Visuals:

Support your descriptions with high-quality images or videos, providing a richer understanding of your product.

SEO-friendly Keywords:

Integrate relevant keywords naturally. Avoid keyword stuffing, which can detract from the readability and appeal of your descriptions.

Remember, creating compelling product descriptions is a dynamic process. Continuously refine them based on customer feedback and data for constant improvement. Let your creativity flow while maintaining a polished and professional tone.

Selecting the Right Tags and Categories

In Etsy's marketplace, the right tags and categories are instrumental in boosting your product's visibility and attracting potential buyers.

Tags:

Choose tags that reflect your potential customers' search terms. Consider style, colour, material, and unique features. For example, tags for a handmade ceramic mug with a floral design might include 'ceramic mug', 'floral design', 'handmade', 'gift for her', and 'unique home decor'.

When selecting tags, balance broad terms with specific ones. Broad terms might attract a wider audience but face more competition, while specific tags can target more intent-driven customers.

Categories:

Categories help buyers navigate the marketplace. Select the most relevant primary category for your product, like 'Jewellery' or 'Accessories' for handmade jewellery. Add up to two related secondary categories to refine your product's classification further.

Choosing the right categories increases the likelihood of appearing in relevant search results, drawing the attention of your target audience. Selecting appropriate tags and categories is a vital step in optimising your Etsy listings, improving SEO performance, and attracting potential buyers.

Chapter 4: Mastering the Visuals

The Importance of High-Quality Images

As an Etsy seller, you're acutely aware that images are paramount in attracting potential buyers and driving sales. Indeed, high-quality images significantly influence the overall SEO performance of your Etsy listings, a fact I've personally witnessed.

When it comes to SEO, images greatly enhance your listing's visibility in search results. Etsy's search algorithm considers various factors, including image quality, relevance, and customer engagement. Investing in high-quality images is essential if you aim to achieve higher rankings and stand out from the competition.

Investing in high-quality images is essential if you aim to achieve higher rankings and stand out from the competition.

You may wonder, what constitutes a high-quality image? It transcends mere resolution or clarity. It involves capturing the essence of your product and presenting it in a visually appealing manner. Professional-looking images that highlight the unique features, details, and benefits of your product will attract potential buyers and boost the likelihood of conversion.

But professionalism isn't the only consideration. Infusing your images with a sense of fun can significantly enhance your connection with your target audience. Depending on your product, experiment with different settings, props, or even models to inject personality and forge an emotional bond with your customers. After all, buyers are more inclined to purchase from sellers with whom they feel a connection.

Optimising your product images for SEO involves striking the right balance in image specifications, such as size, resolution, and file format. Oversized images can slow down page load speeds, adversely affecting SEO. Conversely, images that are too small or of low resolution might not provide sufficient detail for informed buying decisions.

The choice of file format is also crucial. JPEG is widely used for product images, balancing quality with file size. However, for transparent backgrounds or preserving high-quality details, PNG or TIFF formats may be more appropriate.

Lastly, don't overlook the importance of alt text and image descriptions. They provide essential metadata, assisting search engines in understanding and indexing your images. Be descriptive and include relevant keywords in your alt text to enhance your listing's SEO performance and visibility.

In conclusion, high-quality images are transformative in Etsy SEO. They capture potential buyers' attention and increase your listing's search result visibility. Invest in images that showcase your product's unique features and personality, and optimise image specifications for enhanced SEO and page load speed. The effort is certainly worth it!

Using Videos to Enhance Your Listings

As an Etsy seller eager to boost your listings and SEO performance, consider the game-changing potential of incorporating videos. Videos not only engage and captivate potential buyers but also significantly impact your search visibility. Let's explore the benefits of using videos to enhance your Etsy listings.

Videos on Etsy provide a dynamic and visually appealing product showcase. They offer potential buyers a more immersive experience, allowing them to better understand your product's features and details. Studies suggest that videos achieve higher click-through rates than images alone, thereby enhancing your chances of making a sale.

Creating compelling videos involves storytelling. Show viewers how your product can solve a problem or enhance their lifestyle. The video is your opportunity to display creativity, unique selling points, and the value your product offers.

Keep your videos concise yet impactful, ideally around 30 seconds to 1 minute, and include a call-to-action, encouraging viewers to visit your Etsy shop or make a purchase.

Optimise your video for Etsy's search visibility. Start with an attention-grabbing title incorporating relevant keywords. Write a compelling description providing additional product information and benefits, and use relevant keywords that potential buyers might search for. Consider adding links to your Etsy shop or specific product listings to drive traffic and conversions.

Tags are crucial in enhancing your video's search visibility. Use relevant keywords and phrases as tags, helping Etsy's search algorithm understand your video's content and align it with user queries.

Image SEO: Beyond the Aesthetics

Optimizing your product images for SEO is about more than just visual appeal. The metadata you include, particularly in the context of Etsy, plays a crucial role. This encompasses the alt text, file names, and descriptions that accompany your images, all of which contribute to improving your product's visibility and search performance on Etsy.

Alt Text:

Purpose: Alt text is a brief, descriptive text displayed when an image can't load or for users with visual impairments. It's crucial for both accessibility and SEO.

Example: For a handmade necklace, alt text could be "Handmade freshwater pearl necklace with gold clasp," accurately describing the image while including relevant keywords.

Image File Names:

Purpose: Image file names help search engines understand what your image is about. Using descriptive, keyword-rich file names can improve your images' SEO relevance.

To add a text alternative to your listing images:

Sign in to Etsy.com and go to **Shop Manager.**

- Select **Listings.**

- Select a listing.

- Hover over the photo you want to add alternative text to.

- Select the pencil icon.

- Type your alternative text in the box underneath the image.

- Choose **Save.**

You can add a description for as many images as you want.

Example: Instead of a generic file name like IMG_12345.jpg, use a descriptive name such as "bohemian-style-handmade-necklace.jpg" for a Bohemian style handmade necklace.

Etsy Description and Tags:

Purpose: Etsy allows you to add a description and tags to each listing, which are vital components of your SEO strategy. This metadata helps Etsy's algorithm understand and categorize your product.

Description Example: For a vintage dress, the description could detail the era, style, and material, like "1950s vintage polka dot dress, perfect for summer, made from breathable cotton fabric."

Tag Example: Tags for the same dress could include "vintage summer dress," "1950s polka dot dress," "retro cotton dress."

Remember, while crafting your Etsy descriptions, focus on incorporating keywords naturally. Avoid keyword stuffing as it can make your descriptions less appealing to potential buyers. The goal is to provide clear, descriptive, and engaging content that also aligns with what your target audience might be searching for.

By paying attention to these aspects of image SEO - alt text, image file names, and Etsy-specific metadata like descriptions and tags - you can enhance the visibility, searchability, and accessibility of your product images. This not only helps your products rank better in Etsy's search results but also provides a better experience for your potential customers, leading to improved engagement and sales.

Chapter 5:
Pricing Strategies for Better Ranking

How pricing affects Etsy SEO

Optimising your Etsy shop for better search rankings significantly involves pricing strategies. It requires a careful balance between setting competitive prices to attract customers and considering the impact on your search ranking. Let's delve into how pricing affects Etsy SEO and explore strategies for achieving an optimal balance.

Pricing influences search rankings on Etsy because it directly affects your shop's conversion rate. Etsy's search algorithm uses conversion rates as a key metric to gauge the relevance and popularity of your products. A higher conversion rate indicates that your products are meeting customer expectations, which can, in turn, improve your search ranking.

For instance, if you are selling handmade jewellery and set your prices higher than your competitors, aiming to maximise profits, this could result in a lower conversion rate if customers find the prices too high. Consequently, your search ranking might suffer

Etsy's search algorithm uses conversion rates as a key metric to gauge the relevance and popularity of your products.

as Etsy's algorithm could interpret the lower conversion rate as an indication of lesser relevance or popularity.

Conversely, pricing your products too low might initially attract customers but could signal to Etsy that your products are of lower quality, which may also negatively affect your search ranking.

Striking the right balance involves researching and analysing the pricing strategies of your competitors. Understand the market price range for similar products to make informed pricing decisions. Consider factors like materials, craftsmanship, and the uniqueness of your products when setting your prices.

Pay attention to your performance metrics, too. Etsy offers valuable data on conversion rates, sales volume, and customer feedback. Use this data to inform your pricing adjustments. For example, if your conversion rate is low relative to competitors, consider tweaking your prices to see if this positively influences your conversion rate and, consequently, your search ranking.

Remember, finding the ideal price point is an ongoing process. Continuously monitor and analyse your shop's performance metrics, making necessary adjustments to remain competitive and optimise your Etsy SEO. This approach ensures that your pricing strategy not only meets market expectations but also supports your shop's overall search visibility and success.

Balancing Competitiveness and Profitability

Finding the right balance between competitiveness and profitability on Etsy is crucial. You need to offer competitive pricing to attract customers and boost your search rankings, while also ensuring that your profit margins are healthy. This subchapter explores strategies to achieve both competitiveness and profitability.

Strategy 1: Bundle Products

Bundling products is an effective way to optimise your profit margins while maintaining competitive prices. By creating sets of related items, you increase the overall value for the customer and maximise your profits. For instance, if you sell handmade jewellery, consider offering a bundle that includes a necklace, earrings, and a bracelet at a slightly reduced price compared to buying each item separately. This approach allows you to offer an attractive price point while driving higher profits.

Strategy 2: Focus on High-Margin Products

Another strategy is to concentrate on high-margin products in your Etsy shop. Review your product catalogue to identify items with the highest profit margins. These should be the products you focus on marketing and optimising for search rankings. By dedicating more effort to these high-margin products, you can remain competitive in pricing while maximising your profitability.

Strategy 3: Streamline Your Operations

Optimising your operational processes can also aid in improving profit margins. Look for opportunities to streamline and cut costs without sacrificing quality. For example, bulk purchasing materials or finding more efficient packaging and shipping methods can reduce overhead costs, allowing you to maintain competitive pricing while increasing profits.

BALANCING COMPETITIVENESS AND PROFITABILITY
Utilise Etsy's tools and analytics to optimise your profit margins.

You need to offer competitive pricing to attract customers and boost your search rankings, while also ensuring that your profit margins are healthy.

Strategy 4: Offer Limited-Time Promotions

Limited-time promotions are an effective way to boost sales and attract new customers without undermining your overall pricing strategy. You could offer discounts on select products for a limited period or create special promotions for holidays or events. Such promotions create a sense of urgency and exclusivity, driving sales while keeping pricing competitive in the long term.

Strategy 5: Leverage Etsy's Tools and Insights

Utilise Etsy's tools and analytics to optimise your profit margins. Etsy provides valuable data on trends, customer behaviour, and pricing strategies. Leveraging these insights helps you make informed decisions about your pricing, allowing you to stay competitive while enhancing profitability.

Achieving the right balance between competitiveness and profitability on Etsy requires strategic planning and ongoing assessment. By implementing these strategies and staying abreast of market trends, you can enjoy the benefits of increased sales and search visibility while maximising your profits.

Price Testing for Optimal Placement

Achieving optimal placement in Etsy's search results is crucial for your success on the platform, and price testing is a highly effective strategy to enhance your competitive edge. This subchapter will delve into the significance of price testing and how it can influence your visibility in search results.

Why is Price Testing Important?

Price testing is essential because your pricing strategy can significantly impact your Etsy success. It enables you to evaluate how different price points affect your conversion rates and sales. This process is key to finding the ideal balance that attracts customers and maintains profitability.

Price testing provides insights into customer behaviour and preferences, revealing the price points at which customers are more inclined to make purchases. This knowledge allows you to adjust your pricing strategy to maximise revenue effectively.

Conducting A/B Testing for Pricing Strategies

A/B testing involves comparing different pricing approaches to see which performs better in terms of sales and SEO optimisation. It's important to keep other variables constant, such as product descriptions and images, to accurately assess the impact of price changes.

For instance, if you're selling handmade jewellery, you might test two pricing options – option A at £25 and option B at £30. Assign half of your customers to see option A and the other half to see option B, then monitor the conversion rates and sales for each option. This approach can reveal which pricing strategy is more effective, guiding your future pricing decisions.

Analysing the Impact of Price Changes

Once you identify a successful pricing strategy, it's crucial to periodically review and adjust it. Analyse how price changes affect customer behaviour and search result visibility. Monitoring conversion rates and sales before and after price adjustments can provide valuable insights.

Utilise Etsy's analytics tools for a deeper understanding of the impact of price changes. These tools offer data on page views, click-through rates, and conversion rates, aiding in data-driven decision-making to optimise your listings for maximum visibility and profitability.

In summary, price testing is a key strategy for optimal search result placement on Etsy. It allows you to understand customer behaviour, identify the most effective pricing strategy, and make informed decisions. By engaging in A/B testing and continuously analysing the impact of price changes, you can fine-tune your pricing, attract more customers, and enhance your Etsy SEO. Start experimenting with different pricing strategies and observe how your Etsy shop grows and prospers.

Chapter 6:
Leveraging Customer Reviews and Feedback

Encouraging positive reviews

Positive customer reviews are a crucial factor in the success of your Etsy shop. They not only offer social proof and build trust among potential customers, but they also significantly contribute to enhancing your shop's SEO performance and boosting sales.

Actively encouraging positive reviews from your satisfied customers is essential. Here are some strategies to help you garner more positive reviews and bolster your shop's reputation on Etsy:

Deliver Exceptional Customer Service:

Providing outstanding customer service is fundamental to receiving positive reviews. Promptly address all inquiries, ensure orders are swiftly dispatched, and make

Actively encouraging positive reviews from your satisfied customers is essential.

customers feel valued and appreciated throughout their shopping experience.

Send Follow-Up Emails:

After customers receive their orders, consider sending a follow-up email to express your gratitude. Encourage them to leave a review if they are satisfied with their purchase. Include a direct link to your shop's review page for their convenience.

Incentivise Reviews:

Offer a small discount or a future coupon code to customers who leave a positive review. This approach motivates them to share their experiences and increases the likelihood of receiving more positive feedback.

Highlight Positive Reviews:

Feature your positive reviews prominently on your shop's homepage or within product listings. This not only serves as social proof but also underscores the value of reviews to potential customers, encouraging them to leave their feedback.

Engage with Your Customers:

Actively connect with your customers through social media, blog posts, or newsletters. Fostering a strong rapport with your audience can lead to more positive reviews and strengthen customer loyalty.

Implementing these strategies can significantly boost the number of positive reviews for your Etsy shop. Remember, a satisfied customer is more likely to leave a review and recommend your shop to others, leading to increased visibility, enhanced reputation, and higher sales volumes. Creating a positive customer experience is key to encouraging reviews that reflect the quality and appeal of your products and services.

Handling Negative Feedback Professionally

Dealing with negative feedback is a part of being an Etsy seller. While it can be challenging to receive criticism, negative feedback can be a valuable source of insight, offering you the chance to improve and positively impact your Etsy SEO.

So, how can you extract valuable insights from negative feedback? Here are a few tips:

Approach Feedback with an Open Mind:

Viewing negative feedback as a growth opportunity is crucial. Try to objectively evaluate the criticism without becoming defensive.

Look for Patterns:

If multiple customers highlight the same issue, it's a strong indicator that improvement is needed. Identifying and addressing these patterns should be a priority.

Ask for Clarification:

If feedback is vague, don't hesitate to reach out to the customer for more specifics. This can help you understand their concerns more clearly and find appropriate solutions.

Quantify the Impact:

Assess the actual impact of negative feedback on your business. Look at metrics like conversion rates, sales, and customer retention to gauge its significance.

While it can be challenging to receive criticism, negative feedback can be a valuable source of insight, offering you the chance to improve.

Experiment with Improvements:

Once you've identified areas for improvement, experiment with different approaches, whether it's tweaking product descriptions, adjusting pricing, or enhancing customer service. Monitor the impact of these changes on your Etsy SEO.

Remember, negative feedback is not a refection of your worth as a seller. Instead, it's an opportunity to learn and grow. Embrace the feedback, make improvements, and watch how it positively impacts your Etsy SEO.

Now that you know how to extract valuable insights from negative feedback, let's focus on how to respond to it effectively. Crafting professional and constructive responses is crucial to maintaining a positive image and mitigating its impact on your SEO.

Here are some tips for responding to negative feedback professionally:

Respond Promptly:

Aim to respond to negative feedback within 24 hours. A quick response demonstrates that you take customer concerns seriously.

Maintain a Polite Tone:

Regardless of the feedback's nature, always respond calmly and professionally. Avoid defensiveness or arguments.

Show Empathy:

Acknowledge the customer's concerns and apologise for any inconvenience. This shows you value their feedback and are committed to resolving issues.

Offer a Solution:

Where possible, offer a solution or workaround. This proactive approach can turn a negative experience into a positive one.

Take the Conversation Offline:

If the issue requires further discussion or resolution, provide contact information for the customer to reach out privately. This prevents public back-and-forth and shows that you're committed to resolving the issue.

By responding to negative feedback professionally, you not only maintain a positive image on Etsy but also show potential customers that you care about their satisfaction.

Harnessing Reviews for SEO Improvement

When improving your Etsy SEO, customer reviews are incredibly valuable. They provide social proof to potential buyers and significantly boost your shop's search rankings. In this section, we'll explore how to harness customer reviews to optimize your shop's SEO.

One straightforward way to enhance your shop's SEO is by leveraging keywords from customer reviews. Analyze the reviews to identify relevant keywords, and incorporate these into your shop's titles, tags, and product descriptions. For example, if several customers comment on the 'amazing scent' of your handmade candles, use this phrase in your product descriptions to draw more organic traffic.

Customer testimonials are potent social proof that can influence potential buyers. Include positive testimonials in your product listings to boost credibility and improve SEO. Select testimonials that highlight specific benefits or features of your products. If a customer praises your handmade jewellery for its style and durability, feature this testimonial prominently in your listing.

Engaging with customers by responding to their reviews shows appreciation and strengthens your shop's SEO. Include relevant keywords in your responses to positive reviews. This adds keyword-rich content to your listings, enhancing search rankings. Moreover, professionally addressing negative reviews can mitigate their impact on your SEO.

Encouraging ongoing reviews from customers is crucial for continuous SEO improvement. Consider implementing a system that incentivizes reviews, such as offering a discount code or free shipping. Sending follow-up emails after purchases, politely asking for feedback, can also increase the number of reviews.

Here are five examples of texts you can send to customers to encourage them to leave a review:

"Thank you for purchasing from [Shop Name]! We hope you love your new [Product]. Could you spare a moment to share your experience in a review? It helps us immensely and guides fellow shoppers too."

"We noticed you've recently received your [Product]. We'd be thrilled if you could leave us a review on Etsy. As a small shop, your feedback makes all the difference!"

"Hello from [Shop Name]! Did your [Product] brighten your day? If so, we'd love to hear about it. Your review not only supports us but also helps other customers in their choice."

"Thank you for choosing [Shop Name] for your [Product]. If you're satisfied with your purchase, please consider leaving us a review. As a token of our gratitude, here's a [Discount Code] for your next order!"

"We hope your [Product] is everything you hoped for! Sharing your thoughts in a review helps our small business grow and serves our community. Plus, we'd love to hear what you think!"

By using these strategies, you can significantly enhance your Etsy shop's SEO performance. Customer reviews not only boost SEO but also build trust and credibility with your audience, giving your shop a competitive edge.

Chapter 7:
SEO-Friendly Shop Policies

Creating policies that boost SEO

Creating shop policies that satisfy customers and enhance your SEO performance is a smart strategy for any Etsy seller. In this section, I'll guide you through crafting SEO-friendly shop policies that align with Etsy's guidelines while boosting your shop's visibility.

Tip #1: Use Relevant Keywords

Incorporating relevant keywords into your shop policies can significantly improve your SEO. If you sell handmade jewellery, for example, weave in terms like 'handcrafted jewellery', 'unique jewellery', or 'artisanal jewellery'. This increases the likelihood of your shop showing up in searches for these specific terms.

Incorporating relevant keywords into your shop policies can significantly improve your SEO.

Tip #2: Be Clear and Concise

Clarity and conciseness are crucial in your shop policies. While including keywords is important, avoid jargon or overly complex language that could confuse your customers. Opt for simple, straightforward language that effectively communicates your policies.

Tip #3: Address Common Concerns

Anticipate and address potential customer concerns in your policies. If you offer international shipping, for instance, detail shipping times, customs fees, and tracking options. This approach not only assists your customers but also establishes you as a considerate and reliable seller.

Tip #4: Showcase Your Unique Selling Proposition

Your shop policies are more than just rules; they're an opportunity to highlight what sets your shop apart. Is it your dedication to customer satisfaction, your eco-friendly packaging, or perhaps your prompt responses to enquiries? Use your policies to showcase these unique aspects, making your shop more attractive to potential customers and improving your SEO.

Regularly updating your shop policies is essential as your business grows and customer expectations evolve. Keeping your policies up-to-date ensures they continue to meet customer needs and support your shop's SEO strategy.

Next, let's explore the specifics of how these tips can be implemented effectively in your shop policies on Etsy, ensuring they not only adhere to best practices but also contribute positively to your shop's overall SEO performance.

The Impact of Shipping Times on Search Ranking

Etsy SEO can significantly influence the success of your shop, and a key factor in Etsy's search algorithm is shipping times. Quicker shipping can lead to a higher search ranking. In this section, we'll explore the impact of shipping times on search ranking and how you can optimise this aspect of your shop to enhance your SEO performance on Etsy.

Understanding how shipping times affect your search ranking is crucial for optimising your shop effectively. When customers search for products on Etsy, the platform considers various factors, including shipping times, to determine search results. Etsy aims to ensure customers have a positive shopping experience with timely order receipt, thus prioritising shops with faster shipping in their search rankings.

Consider this scenario: a customer searches for a specific product available in multiple shops. If your shop has longer shipping times compared to others, those with faster shipping are likely to rank higher in the search results. This makes it more probable for potential customers to see and select these shops over yours. Conversely, offering faster shipping times enhances your chance of ranking higher, increasing your shop's visibility.

Now that we understand the importance of shipping times in Etsy SEO, let's look at strategies to optimise your shipping times and boost your shop's SEO performance:

Offer Same-Day or Next-Day Shipping:

Providing expedited shipping options can significantly enhance your search ranking. Customers appreciate fast shipping, and Etsy recognises this. By offering same-day or next-day shipping, you can distinguish your shop from competitors and improve your chances of appearing higher in search results. Partner with reliable carriers to ensure timely delivery.

Streamline Your Order Processing:

Efficient order processing minimises shipping delays. Keep your inventory current to avoid order fulfilment delays. Establish efficient packaging and labelling processes to expedite shipping readiness.

Use Shipping Labels and Trackable Packages:

Shipping labels and trackable packages not only streamline your shipping operations but also provide a positive customer experience. Trackable packages give customers confidence and satisfaction, potentially leading to positive reviews and an improved search ranking for your shop.

Optimise International Shipping:

If offering international shipping, optimising this aspect can enhance your global competitiveness. Explore international shipping options, understand customs requirements, and provide accurate delivery time estimates. Utilising international shipping software or partnering with specialist carriers can help streamline this process.

Communicate Clear Shipping Expectations:

Clear communication regarding shipping is vital. Explicitly state processing times, shipping methods, and delivery estimates in your product listings to manage customer expectations and reduce potential conflicts. It's always preferable to under-promise and over-deliver.

By adopting these strategies, you can optimise your shipping times and enhance your Etsy search ranking. Remember, customers value prompt shipping, and Etsy rewards shops that provide this service efficiently. Evaluate and adjust your shipping processes as needed, and observe how your SEO performance improves.

Balancing Customer Expectations and SEO Needs

Achieving a balance between meeting customer expectations and optimising your Etsy shop for SEO is essential for success. This subchapter discusses how to create shop policies that satisfy customers while boosting your visibility on Etsy.

One effective approach is thorough keyword research. Identify keywords relevant to your products and incorporate them into your policies. For instance, if selling handmade jewellery, include keywords like 'unique jewellery', 'handcrafted accessories', or 'artisanal earrings'. This not only improves search visibility but also attracts potential customers.

However, keyword integration should not compromise customer satisfaction. Ensure that your policies are clear, concise, and resonate with your audience. While optimising for SEO, prioritise providing valuable information and addressing customer concerns.

Building trust is crucial in balancing customer expectations with SEO needs. Transparency in your policies, particularly regarding shipping and returns, is key. Open and honest communication establishes trust and credibility, positively impacting customer experiences and Etsy SEO. When customers understand and feel confident about your policies, they are more likely to engage with your shop.

Here's an example of a transparent policy that balances customer needs with SEO:

> *"Our shop is committed to delivering an exceptional shopping experience. If you're not completely satisfied with your purchase, please contact us within 7 days of receipt for assistance with returns or exchanges.*

We aim for transparency in our shipping process. Orders are typically processed within 1-2 business days, with standard shipping taking around 3-5 business days and expedited shipping 1-3 business days.

Should your order arrive damaged, please inform us immediately, and we'll promptly address the issue.

Your satisfaction is paramount, and we endeavour to make your experience with us smooth and enjoyable!"

Regularly review and update your shop policies to align with customer feedback and evolving Etsy SEO guidelines. If common questions or concerns arise from customers, consider incorporating answers into your policies. Continuous refinement ensures your policies stay relevant and user-friendly.

Remember, balancing customer expectations with SEO needs is an ongoing process. Be adaptable, make necessary changes, and always prioritise the overall customer experience in your decision-making.

Chapter 8:
Link Building for Etsy Shops

The basics of backlinking

Building high-quality backlinks is crucial for enhancing your Etsy shop's SEO performance. Backlinks not only drive traffic to your shop but also signal to search engines that your shop is reputable and credible. In this section, we'll delve into strategies for building high-quality backlinks that positively impact your shop's SEO on Etsy.

Let's first understand the different types of backlinks that can boost your shop's search visibility on Etsy. Backlinks can take various forms:

Backlinks not only drive traffic to your shop but also signal to search engines that your shop is reputable and credible.

Editorial Backlinks:

These are naturally given by other websites or blogs that find your content valuable.

Guest Blogging Backlinks:

Writing a guest post for another website or blog and including a link back to your Etsy shop creates a backlink.

Social Media Backlinks:

Links from social media platforms like Facebook, Instagram, Twitter, and Pinterest can serve as backlinks, driving traffic to your shop.

Directory Backlinks:

These come from online directories or listings pointing to your Etsy shop.

Forum Backlinks:

Participation in forums with a link to your shop in your forum signature or posts can generate backlinks.

Now that we have a clear understanding of backlinks and their SEO impact, let's dive into the basics of backlinking and how you can start building high-quality backlinks for your Etsy shop.

One of the best ways to attract natural backlinks is by creating content that other websites or blogs would want to share and link back to. Focus on creating high-quality product descriptions, blog posts, or tutorials that provide value to your target audience. The more valuable and shareable your content is, the higher the chances of earning backlinks.

Identify influencers and bloggers in your niche who have a strong online presence. Reach out to them and ofer to collaborate by providing them with a free product sample or by offering an exclusive discount code for their audience. In return, ask them to write a review or feature your product on their website or blog, including a backlink to your Etsy shop.

Look for websites or blogs that are relevant to your Etsy shop and accept guest posts. Pitch them with unique and valuable content ideas that align with their audience's interests. When your guest post gets published, make sure to include a backlink to your shop in your author bio or within the content itself.

8: LINK BUILDING FOR ETSY SHOPS

Use social media platforms to promote your Etsy shop and build backlinks. Engage with your audience, share your products, and encourage social sharing. The more your content gets shared on social media, the higher the chances of earning backlinks from social media platforms.

Join relevant online communities and forums where your target audience hangs out. Engage in discussions, ofer valuable insights, and include a link to your shop in your forum signature. Over time, as you build relationships and establish yourself as an expert in your niche, you'll naturally earn backlinks from forum discussions.

Strategies for Earning Quality Backlinks

Earning quality backlinks for your Etsy shop can significantly enhance visibility, and having a robust strategy is key. Here, we'll discuss effective strategies to help you build high-quality backlinks and boost your shop's presence.

Create Compelling and Shareable Content

One of the most effective methods to earn quality backlinks is by creating content that is both compelling and shareable. This could be informative blog posts, how-to guides, or engaging videos showcasing your products. Providing valuable and unique content increases the chances of others linking back to your shop.

Pro tip: Be creative with your content. For instance, infographics can be a visually appealing way to convey information and attract backlinks.

Collaborate with Influencers and Bloggers

Influencers and bloggers with established audiences can be instrumental in earning quality backlinks. Propose collaborations to those who align with your niche, perhaps by offering them free product samples in return for a review or a feature on their platform.

Pro tip: Personalise your outreach to influencers or bloggers, highlighting the mutual benefits of a collaboration.

Leverage Social Media Platforms

Social media platforms are excellent for earning backlinks and increasing visibility. Engage in relevant communities, share your content, and join discussions. Being an active and valuable community member raises the likelihood of earning backlinks.

Pro tip: Utilise relevant hashtags and engage in trending topics within your niche to discover opportunities for contribution and potential backlinks.

Participate in Online Forums and Communities

Engaging in online forums and communities related to your niche can help build relationships and earn backlinks. Offer answers, insights, and share your expertise authentically to foster connections that may lead to backlinks.

Pro tip: Focus on adding value rather than self-promotion; genuine interaction is key to building relationships in these forums.

Guest Blogging

Guest blogging involves writing articles for other websites in your niche, often in exchange for a backlink to your Etsy shop. Identify reputable websites or blogs that accept guest posts and offer them unique and relevant content ideas.

Pro tip: Ensure your guest post content aligns with the host website's audience and guidelines to increase the likelihood of acceptance.

Network with Other Etsy Sellers

Networking with fellow Etsy sellers can lead to collaborative and backlink opportunities. Engage with sellers offering complementary products and explore reciprocal promotion methods.

Pro tip: Joint giveaways or affiliate partnerships can be effective ways to strengthen collaborations with other Etsy sellers.

Remember, earning quality backlinks is a process that requires patience and consistent effort. Focus on building genuine connections and relationships. These strategies will set you on the path to securing valuable backlinks for your Etsy shop.

Avoiding Common Link-Building Pitfalls

When I first started building backlinks for my Etsy shop's SEO, I was keen to see my shop rise in search rankings and gain more visibility. However, I quickly realised there were common link-building pitfalls to avoid for long-term success. Here are some insights on how to build effective backlinks for your Etsy shop while avoiding these mistakes.

A frequent error many Etsy sellers make is prioritising quantity over quality in backlinks. It's tempting to think more backlinks will automatically enhance SEO, but the truth is that the quality of backlinks is far more important. Focus on creating high-quality, relevant backlinks that genuinely benefit your shop, rather than amassing a large number of lesser-quality links.

Another pitfall is over-reliance on reciprocal link exchanges. While exchanging links with other Etsy sellers might seem a quick way to build backlinks, this method is less effective than before. Modern search engines can easily identify reciprocal link schemes. Instead, aim for one-way backlinks from authoritative, relevant websites, as these are more valuable and improve your shop's SEO.

Regarding anchor text, some Etsy sellers use generic phrases or keywords, such as 'click here' or 'learn more'. These don't provide context to search engines about your shop's content. Use descriptive anchor text with relevant keywords instead. For example, if your shop specialises in handmade jewellery, consider using 'handmade jewellery shop' or 'unique jewellery designs' as anchor texts.

Lastly, a common mistake is failing to diversify backlink sources. A varied backlink profile is crucial. If most of your backlinks come from a single source, it may appear suspicious to search engines and negatively affect your shop's SEO. Ensure you diversify your backlinks, obtaining them from a variety of sources like authoritative websites, blogs, social media platforms, and online directories.

By avoiding these common link-building pitfalls, you can establish a strong and effective backlink profile for your Etsy shop. Remember: quality over quantity, focus on one-way backlinks, use descriptive anchor texts, and diversify your backlink sources. These guidelines will help enhance your shop's SEO and boost its visibility in search rankings.

Chapter 9:
Seasonal and Trend-Based SEO

Anticipating seasonal trends for better visibility

To boost your Etsy shop's SEO performance, it's crucial to identify and capitalise on seasonal search trends. Incorporating these trends into your marketing strategy enhances visibility during peak periods, attracting more customers to your shop.

Staying ahead with seasonal trends is vital for enhancing your shop's visibility. Analyse search trends and patterns from previous years to understand what customers seek during specific seasons and holidays. This insight helps you optimise your listings and target relevant keywords to draw potential buyers.

For instance, suppose you sell handmade holiday ornaments. Analysing search trends might reveal that searches for 'personalised Christmas ornaments' begin to rise in October and peak in November. With this knowledge, optimise

> *Analyse search trends and patterns from previous years to understand what customers seek during specific seasons and holidays.*

your listings with keywords like 'personalised Christmas ornaments' to boost search result appearances during this period.

Consider another example: if you sell clothing items, you might find that searches for 'summer dresses' spike in May and June. Align your listings with these keywords and create content related to summer fashion to tap into this trend and attract shoppers seeking summer attire.

Here's a list of examples of seasonal search trends:

Christmas - Increased searches for gifts, decorations, festive attire, and seasonal crafts.

Halloween - Higher interest in costumes, decorations, themed party supplies, and spooky crafts.

Valentine's Day - A spike in searches for romantic gifts, jewellery, special experiences, and personalised items.

Mother's Day - Elevated searches for gifts, flowers, handmade items, and sentimental keepsakes.

Summer - Increased interest in summer clothing, beach accessories, travel essentials, and outdoor products.

Winter - Higher searches for warm clothing, heating accessories, holiday decorations, and winter sports gear.

Easter - A rise in searches for Easter decorations, crafts, baskets, and chocolate gifts.

Thanksgiving - Elevated interest in cookware, table decorations, festive food items, and hosting essentials.

Black Friday - High searches for deals, electronics, clothing sales, and early Christmas shopping.

Cyber Monday - Continued interest in online deals, tech gadgets, fashion sales, and unique online finds.

Spring - Increased searches for gardening tools, spring cleaning products, outdoor furniture, and light apparel.

Autumn/Fall - Elevated interest in fall decorations, warm clothing, Halloween items, and back-to-school products.

New Year's - A spike in searches for party supplies, calendars, planners, fitness gear, and self-improvement items.

Father's Day - Higher interest in gifts for dads, gadgets, personalised items, and experience gifts.

Back-to-School - Increased searches for school supplies, clothing, educational tools, and dorm essentials.

Wedding Season (usually spring/summer) - Elevated searches for wedding attire, decorations, gifts, and planning tools.

St. Patrick's Day - Higher interest in green-themed attire, decorations, and party supplies.

Chinese New Year - Increased searches for traditional attire, decorations, gifts, and food items.

Balancing proactivity and reactivity is crucial when anticipating seasonal trends. While historical data offers valuable insights, it's essential to monitor current trends and adapt your SEO strategy accordingly. This might involve keeping an eye on social media trends, popular hashtags, and staying abreast of current events and holidays that may influence search behaviours.

By anticipating seasonal trends and tailoring your listings accordingly, you can significantly improve your shop's visibility and attract more customers during peak times. Regularly analyse and update your SEO strategy to remain relevant and seize new opportunities.

Updating Listings with Trend-Based Optimizations

As an Etsy seller, it's essential to keep your listings updated with trend-based optimizations to stay relevant in the ever-evolving market. By incorporating the latest trends into your product descriptions, titles, and tags, you can enhance your SEO and attract more potential customers. Here are some tips to help you update your listings with trend-based optimizations:

1. Stay up-to-date with the latest trends:

One of the first steps in updating your listings is to research and understand the current trends in your niche. Stay connected with industry blogs, social media platforms, and relevant forums to keep track of what's hot at the moment. Look for keywords and phrases that are gaining popularity and align with your products.

For example, if you sell handmade jewellery, you might notice that minimalist designs are currently trending. In this case, you could update your product descriptions to highlight the minimalistic nature of your jewellery or incorporate keywords like minimalist jewellery or simple and elegant.

2. Analyze competitor listings:

Take a look at your competitors' listings and identify the keywords and phrases they are using. Pay attention to their titles, descriptions, and tags to get an idea of what is currently working in your niche. While it's important to differentiate yourself, analyzing your competitors can help you understand which trends are popular and provide inspiration for updates to your own listings.

For instance, if you notice that a lot of your competitors are using the term boho-chic in their listings, you might consider incorporating that term into your own product titles or tags if it aligns with your brand and products.

3. Optimize your titles and descriptions:

Updating your titles and descriptions is crucial for attracting organic traffic from search engines. Incorporate the trending keywords and phrases you've identified into your titles and product descriptions in a natural and compelling way.

For example, if you're selling handmade candles and discover that soy candles is a trending keyword, you could update your title to include Hand-poured Soy Candles for a Relaxing Atmosphere and incorporate soy candles naturally in your description.

4. Experiment with tags:

Tags play an important role in Etsy's search algorithm. Experiment with different combinations of tags that include trending keywords to improve your chances of appearing in relevant search results.

Continuing with the handmade candle example, you might consider using tags like soy candle, relaxation candles, hand-poured candles, or aromatherapy candles, depending on the specific features and benefits of your product.

5. Test, analyze, and iterate:

Once you've updated your listings with trend-based optimizations, regularly monitor their performance and make adjustments as needed. Pay attention to the click-through rates, conversion rates, and keyword rankings to determine what is working and what needs improvement.

Remember, trends can change quickly, so it's important to stay flexible and adapt your listings accordingly. Continuously updating your listings with trend-based optimizations will help you maintain a competitive edge in search rankings and attract the right customers to your Etsy shop.

Balance the need for seasonal optimizations with the importance of maintaining evergreen SEO practices by creating high-quality, timeless content.

Maintaining evergreen SEO among seasonal changes

When it comes to maintaining consistent visibility and search rankings on Etsy, evergreen SEO strategies are an absolute must. These strategies are designed to withstand the test of time, ensuring that your shop remains relevant and visible to potential customers regardless of the season.

So, how do you balance the need for seasonal optimizations with the importance of maintaining evergreen SEO practices? It's all about finding the right balance and understanding which strategies work best for your shop.

One key aspect of maintaining evergreen SEO among seasonal changes is to focus on creating high-quality, timeless content. This means producing content that remains valuable and relevant to your target audience regardless of the time of year. For example, if you sell handmade jewellery, you could create a blog post about the different gemstones used in your pieces and their meanings. This type of content will continue to attract organic traffic and engagement throughout the year, regardless of seasonal trends.

Another important factor to consider is keyword research. While seasonal keywords can certainly be beneficial for driving traffic during specific times of the year, it's crucial not to neglect the importance of evergreen keywords. These are the keywords that accurately represent your products and stay relevant over time. By incorporating a healthy mix of both seasonal and evergreen keywords in your SEO strategy, you can attract both short-term and long-term traffic to your Etsy shop.

Furthermore, it's essential to regularly review and update your SEO strategies to adapt to evolving seasonal trends while maintaining long-term SEO effectiveness. Start by analyzing data from previous seasons to identify patterns and trends. For example, if you notice that certain products or categories perform exceptionally well during specific seasons, you can optimize your content and keywords accordingly.

Additionally, staying active on social media platforms can also help you maintain evergreen SEO among seasonal changes. By regularly sharing your evergreen content and keeping your followers engaged, you can drive traffic to your Etsy shop and increase your chances of ranking well in search results.

Overall, maintaining evergreen SEO among seasonal changes requires a combination of strategic planning, keyword research, timeless content creation, and staying active on social media. By striking the right balance between seasonal optimizations and evergreen SEO practices, you can ensure consistent visibility and search rankings for your Etsy shop throughout the year.

Chapter 10:
Using Social Media to Boost Etsy SEO

Social signals and their impact on SEO

When it comes to optimizing your Etsy shop for search engine optimization (SEO), there are many factors to consider. One often overlooked aspect is the role of social signals. Social signals refer to the likes, shares, and comments that your shop receives on social media platforms.

Why are social signals important for your Etsy shop's SEO? Well, search engines like Google and Etsy's internal search algorithm take into account various signals to determine the credibility, authority, and relevance of a website or online store. And when it comes to Etsy, social signals can play a significant role in boosting your shop's visibility and rankings.

Think about it - if your products are receiving a lot of likes, shares, and comments on social

Social signals refer to the likes, shares, and comments that your shop receives on social media platforms.

LEVERAGE SOCIAL SIGNALS
Ensure your social media profiles are complete and consistent with your Etsy brand.

media, it indicates that people are interested in what you have to ofer. This engagement signals to search engines that your shop is trustworthy and popular among potential buyers.

Imagine you're a customer looking for unique handmade jewellery on Etsy. You come across two similar shops, but one has hundreds of likes, shares, and positive comments on their social media posts, while the other has little to no engagement. Which shop would you consider more credible and appealing? Most likely, you'd lean towards the one with the social proof.

So, how can you optimize your social media profiles to leverage these social signals and enhance your shop's SEO on Etsy? Let's dive into some tips and techniques:

Ensure your social media profiles are complete and consistent with your Etsy brand. Use your shop name as the handle and include a link to your Etsy shop in the bio or website section.

Create engaging content that showcases your products and resonates with your target audience. Encourage followers to like, share, and comment on your posts by asking questions or prompting them to tag their friends.

Use relevant keywords in your social media posts and descriptions to make it easier for search engines to understand the context and relevance of your content. For example, if you sell handmade candles, include keywords like handmade candles, natural candles, or soy wax candles in your posts.

Engage with your followers by responding to comments, thanking them for their support, and addressing any inquiries or concerns promptly. Building a strong and engaged community on social media will not only improve your shop's SEO but also create a loyal customer base.

Collaborate with influencers or micro-influencers in your niche to amplify your reach and gain more social signals. Look for individuals or accounts with a significant following and a genuine interest in your products. By partnering with them, you can tap into their audience and potentially generate more likes, shares, and comments.

Remember, optimization is an ongoing process, and it takes time and consistent efort to build your social media presence. But by incorporating these strategies into your marketing plan, you can harness the power of social signals to support your Etsy shop's SEO and attract more potential customers.

Integrating your Etsy shop with social platforms

Integrating your Etsy shop with social platforms is a crucial step in maximizing your online presence and reaching a wider audience. By linking your Etsy shop with your social media accounts, you can seamlessly promote your products, drive traffic, and boost your search engine optimization (SEO).

One of the key strategies to consider when integrating your Etsy shop with social platforms is cross-promotion. By leveraging different social media platforms, you can engage with a diverse range of users and increase the visibility of your Etsy shop. Let's take a closer look at some effective cross-promotion strategies for various social media platforms:

Facebook:

Create a dedicated Facebook Page for your Etsy shop and regularly share posts highlighting your products, promotions, and updates. Join relevant Facebook groups or communities where you can engage with potential customers and share links to your Etsy listings.

Instagram:

Set up an Instagram Business account and showcase your products through visually appealing posts. Utilize popular hashtags that align with your brand and target audience to increase discoverability. Collaborate with influencers or micro-influencers within your niche to reach a wider audience.

Pinterest:

Create boards that feature your Etsy products and curate relevant content. Optimize your pins with keyword-rich descriptions and link them back to your Etsy listings. Join group boards or collaborate with other Pinterest users to expand your reach.

Twitter:

Utilize Twitter to share updates, promotions, and engage with your audience through hashtags and mentions. Participate in relevant Twitter chats or utilize Twitter's Advanced Search feature to find potential customers who are looking for products similar to yours.

LinkedIn:

If your Etsy shop caters to a more professional audience, consider creating a LinkedIn Company Page. Share industry insights, updates, and product launches to establish yourself as an expert in your feld. Connect with other professionals and join relevant groups to expand your network.

TikTok:

Tap into the rising popularity of TikTok by creating short and engaging videos showcasing your products or behind-the-scenes content. Utilize trending challenges or sounds to increase your chances of going viral and gain exposure to a younger demographic.

Remember, the key to successful cross-promotion on social media platforms is to create compelling and shareable content that resonates with your target audience.

Make sure to incorporate your Etsy shop link in your social media profiles, post captions, and call-to-action buttons to drive traffic directly to your listings. Regularly monitor and engage with your social media audience to build a loyal customer base and increase your chances of converting followers into Etsy customers.

By integrating your Etsy shop with social platforms and implementing effective cross-promotion strategies, you can enhance your online visibility, drive organic traffic, and ultimately improve your Etsy SEO and search rankings. So, get creative, have fun, and start leveraging the power of social media to grow your Etsy business!

Creating social content that drives traffic

Crafting engaging social media content is a key strategy to drive traffic to your Etsy shop. With so many users scrolling through their social feeds every day, it's essential to create content that captures their attention and entices them to click through to your shop. In this section, I'm going to share some tips and techniques that have helped me craft compelling and shareable social media content.

First and foremost, it's important to know your audience. Understanding their interests, preferences, and the types of content they engage with will help you tailor your social media posts to resonate with them. Take the time to research and analyze the demographics of your target audience, and use that insight to guide your content creation process. For example, if your Etsy shop specializes in handmade jewellery, your target audience might be young women who are interested in fashion and accessories.

Once you have a clear understanding of your audience, it's time to brainstorm content ideas. Think about what sets your Etsy shop apart from others and how you can showcase that uniqueness through your social media posts. Share behind-the-scenes glimpses of your creative process, feature customer testimonials and reviews, or highlight the inspiration behind your products. The key is to create content that not only promotes your shop but also ofers value or entertainment to your audience.

Visual content is king on social media, so make sure to include eye-catching images and videos in your posts. High-quality, aesthetically pleasing visuals will grab attention and encourage engagement. If you're showcasing a product, consider using lifestyle images that demonstrate how it can be used or styled. You can also create short videos showing your products in action or tutorials on how to use them. Remember, a picture is worth a thousand words, so make sure your visuals are telling a compelling story.

Another effective strategy is to create content that sparks conversation and encourages social sharing. Ask thought-provoking questions, run polls or contests, or invite your audience to share their own experiences or stories related to your products. Not only will this increase engagement, but it will also amplify the reach of your content as users share it with their own networks. People love to be heard and recognized, so giving them a platform to share their thoughts and opinions is a surefire way to drive traffic to your shop.

Lastly, don't forget to optimize your captions and use relevant hashtags. Keywords play a crucial role in SEO (search engine optimization), even on social media platforms. Think about what words or phrases your target audience might be searching for and incorporate them naturally into your captions. In addition, research and use popular hashtags that are relevant to your niche and target audience. This will increase the discoverability of your content and attract users who are interested in what you have to offer.

Chapter 11:
Analyzing Your SEO Performance

Setting up and reading Etsy Shop Stats

In this chapter, we will dive into the exciting world of setting up and reading Etsy Shop Stats. As an Etsy seller, understanding and utilizing this valuable tool is crucial in optimizing your shop's performance and success. Let's get started!

First, let's talk about setting up your Etsy Shop Stats. After signing in to your Etsy account, navigate to the Shop Manager tab and find the Stats section. Here, you will have the option to enable Shop Stats for your shop. Simply click on the Enable button, and Etsy will start collecting data about your shop's performance.

Once you have set up your Etsy Shop Stats, it's time to dive into the key metrics and data points that you should monitor. These metrics will provide valuable insights into the effectiveness of your SEO strategy and help you make informed decisions to improve your shop's visibility and sales.

Understanding and utilizing the Etsy Shop Stats is crucial in optimizing your shop's performance and success.

One important metric to monitor is the Views metric. This metric tells you how many times your listings have been viewed by potential customers. By tracking this metric, you can gauge the effectiveness of your keywords and item descriptions in attracting customers to your shop.

Another essential metric is the Visitors metric. This metric reveals the number of unique visitors to your shop. It gives you an idea of how well your shop is attracting new customers. By analyzing this data, you can identify trends and patterns to optimize your SEO strategy.

Understanding your Top Traffic Sources is also crucial. This metric shows you where your shop's traffic is coming from, such as direct visits, search engine traffic, or social media referrals. By identifying the most significant sources of traffic, you can focus your efforts on channels that bring the most potential customers to your shop.

Now that you have an idea of the key metrics to monitor, let's talk about interpreting and adjusting based on the data obtained from Etsy Shop Stats. It's important to regularly review your data and make informed adjustments to your SEO strategy to improve your shop's performance.

How shoppers found you

Etsy brought 79% of visits

E Etsy app & other Etsy pages	286	↑32%
Etsy search	114	↑18%
Etsy marketing & SEO	20	↑233%

You brought 21% of visits

Direct & other traffic	37	↓3%
Social media ⌄	13	↑18%
Advertising	65	↓28%

For example, if you notice that a particular keyword is driving a significant amount of traffic to your shop, you may want to emphasize that keyword in your item titles, tags, and descriptions. On the other hand, if you find that certain keywords are not performing well, you might consider optimizing or replacing them with more effective ones.

Additionally, take note of any trends or seasonal patterns in your data. This information can help you plan your inventory and promotions to align with customer demand, ultimately maximizing your sales and conversions.

In conclusion, setting up and reading Etsy Shop Stats is an essential aspect of running a successful Etsy shop. By understanding and utilizing the valuable insights provided by Shop Stats, you can optimize your SEO strategy, attract more customers, and ultimately increase your sales. Don't forget to regularly review your data and make informed adjustments to continuously improve your shop's performance.

Happy analyzing!

Using external tools for deeper insights

When it comes to optimizing your Etsy shop's SEO, the native Shop Stats provided by Etsy can undoubtedly give you valuable insights. However, if you're looking to take your SEO analysis to the next level, external SEO analysis tools can provide you with even deeper insights and help you make data-driven decisions to improve your shop's ranking on Etsy.

External tools, such as SEMrush, Moz, and Ahrefs, ofer a plethora of features designed to uncover hidden opportunities and identify areas for improvement in your shop's SEO strategy. Let's take a closer look at some of the techniques and tips for leveraging these tools effectively:

1. Keyword research:

External SEO analysis tools allow you to conduct comprehensive keyword research to identify high-ranking keywords relevant to your shop. By uncovering popular search terms and long-tail keywords with high search volume and low competition, you can optimize your listings and tags for better visibility on Etsy.

For example, let's say you're selling handmade jewellery. Using an external SEO analysis tool, you might discover that the keyword handmade gold earrings has high search volume but relatively low competition. With this insight, you can optimize your listings and tags to include this keyword and potentially attract more organic traffic to your shop.

2. Competitor analysis:

External SEO analysis tools also allow you to analyze your competitors' SEO strategies and identify areas where you can gain a competitive edge. By examining their top-ranking keywords, backlinks, and content strategies, you can gain valuable insights into what's working in your

SEO ANALYSIS TOOLS

Spend time to analyze your competitors' SEO strategies, then implement similar techniques in your shop

niche and apply similar techniques to improve your own shop's SEO performance.

For instance, let's imagine you notice a competitor who consistently ranks high for the keyword boho bracelets. By analyzing their product descriptions, tags, and backlink profile, you may discover that they are leveraging certain strategies, such as including customer reviews and obtaining backlinks from influential bloggers. Armed with this knowledge, you can implement similar techniques in your own shop to boost your rankings for the same keyword.

3. SEO audits:

External SEO analysis tools often provide detailed SEO audits that assess the overall health and performance of your shop's SEO. These audits typically analyze factors such as page load speed, metadata, mobile-friendliness, and internal linking structure, among others.

By conducting regular SEO audits, you can identify and rectify any technical issues that may be hindering your shop's SEO performance. For example, for the ones who owns your own website, the audit might reveal that your shop's load speed is slower than average, leading to a higher bounce rate. Armed with this information, you can optimize your shop's performance by compressing images, minifying CSS and JavaScript, and improving server response time.

4. Backlink analysis:

External SEO analysis tools can also help you evaluate the quality and quantity of backlinks pointing to your shop. Backlinks, or inbound links from other websites, are a key factor in determining your shop's authority and SEO ranking. With the help of these tools, you can identify which websites are linking to your shop, the anchor text used, and assess the overall quality of your backlink profile.

For instance, if you discover that influential blogs or industry websites are linking to your shop, it not only improves your SEO ranking but also increases your shop's credibility and exposure to potential customers. On the other hand, if you find that your backlink profile is primarily composed of low-quality or irrelevant websites, you can take steps to disallow those links and improve the overall quality of your backlink profile.

Overall, external SEO analysis tools can provide valuable insights into your shop's SEO performance on Etsy. By conducting keyword research, analyzing competitors, performing SEO audits, and evaluating backlinks, you can make data-driven decisions and continually optimize your Etsy SEO strategy for better visibility and increased sales.

Adjusting Strategy Based on Performance Metrics

In this section, we will focus on the crucial aspect of adjusting your SEO strategy based on performance metrics. Utilizing Etsy's Shop Stats and other external tools, you can gather valuable data to refine your approach for optimal visibility and sales.

Reviewing Traffic and Engagement Metrics:

Regularly check metrics like page views, visitor numbers, and engagement rates. If certain products or keywords are driving more traffic, consider boosting these in your marketing and SEO efforts.

Assessing Keyword Performance:

Analyse which keywords are bringing in traffic and leading to conversions. If some keywords aren't performing well, it might be time to replace them with more effective ones based on current trends or search analysis.

Evaluating Sales Conversion Rates:

Look at the conversion rates from views to sales. High views but low sales could indicate issues with pricing, product descriptions, or customer trust. Adjust these elements as needed.

Analysing Traffic Sources:

Determine which channels are driving the most traffic to your shop. If social media platforms are major traffic drivers, ramp up your efforts there. If most traffic comes from Etsy search, focus on optimising your Etsy SEO.

Social Media Engagement Analysis:

Monitor the performance of your social media posts. High engagement rates can indicate content that resonates well with your audience, suggesting a similar approach for your Etsy listings.

Customer Feedback and Reviews:

Pay attention to customer feedback. Positive reviews can highlight strengths to capitalise on, while negative feedback can reveal areas for improvement.

Seasonal and Trend Adjustments:

Track seasonal trends impacting your shop. Adjust your inventory, marketing, and SEO strategies to align with these trends for maximised sales during peak seasons.

Competitor Benchmarking:

Keep an eye on competitors' performance. If they are excelling in areas where your shop is lagging, analyse and learn from their strategies.

A/B Testing:

Experiment with different SEO strategies, such as varying keywords, titles, and tags. Monitor the performance of these changes to understand what works best for your shop.

Regular SEO Audits:

Conduct periodic SEO audits using external tools to identify technical areas for improvement like website speed, mobile responsiveness, and image optimization.

By consistently analysing and adjusting your strategy based on performance metrics, you can ensure that your Etsy shop remains competitive and visible in search results, leading to increased traffic and sales.

Chapter 12:
Crafting an SEO-Friendly Shop Layout

Arranging listings for better user experience

When it comes to running an Etsy shop, the layout and arrangement of your listings play a crucial role in both the user experience and the SEO performance. A well-organized shop not only helps your customers find what they need but also improves your search engine rankings. So, let's dive into some tips for arranging your listings to create a better user experience!

A well-organized shop not only helps your customers find what they need but also improves your search engine rankings.

1. Categorize your listings:

Start by categorizing your products into different sections or collections. This helps customers navigate your shop easily and find what they're looking for without any hassle. For example, if you sell handmade jewellery, you can have separate sections for necklaces, earrings, bracelets, and rings. This way, customers can go directly to the section they're interested in.

2. Create clear and concise titles:

Make sure your listing titles are descriptive and concise. Use relevant keywords that potential customers might be searching for. Avoid using vague or ambiguous titles that don't clearly convey what the product is. For example, instead of just Pretty Earrings, use Handmade Silver Hoop Earrings - Minimalist Jewellery.

3. Utilize compelling images:

Invest in high-quality product images that showcase your items in the best possible way. Good images capture attention and entice customers to click on your listings. Make sure to include multiple angles, close-ups, and lifestyle shots whenever applicable. Remember, a picture is worth a thousand words!

4. Optimize your product descriptions:

Your product descriptions should be informative, engaging, and optimized for SEO. Include relevant keywords naturally throughout the description to improve your search rankings. But don't go overboard – prioritize creating valuable content for your customers. Focus on highlighting the unique features, benefits, and usage instructions of your products.

Creating a positive user experience includes providing relevant information, optimizing your shop for SEO, and making the shopping process as smooth as possible.

5. Offer customization options:

Allow customers to personalize or customize their purchases whenever feasible. This adds a personal touch and makes your listings more appealing. For example, if you sell handmade pottery, ofer different color options or the ability to engrave names on the pieces. This customization not only enhances the user experience but also sets you apart from competitors.

6. Provide clear shipping and return policies:

Make sure to clearly communicate your shipping and return policies on each listing. This information helps customers make informed decisions and sets their expectations. Clearly state any shipping costs, estimated delivery times, and the process for returns or exchanges. The transparency builds trust with your customers and encourages them to make a purchase.

Remember, creating a positive user experience is not just about arranging your listings in a visually pleasing way. It's also about providing relevant information, optimizing your shop for SEO, and making the shopping process as smooth as possible. By implementing these tips, you can enhance both the user experience and your shop's SEO performance!

Optimizing your shop's homepage for SEO

As an Etsy seller, one of the most vital aspects of your online shop is the homepage. It serves as the virtual storefront where potential customers land when they visit your shop. Optimizing your shop's homepage for SEO can make a significant impact on attracting organic traffic and improving your search rankings. In this section, we will explore the importance of an SEO-optimized shop homepage and how you can achieve it.

When it comes to creating an SEO-friendly shop homepage, there are several key elements that you need to consider. These elements not only enhance search visibility but also engage your customers. Let's take a closer look at some of the essential elements:

Clear and concise navigation:

Ensure that your homepage has a clear and easy-to-use navigation menu that helps visitors browse through your shop effortlessly. Organize your products into relevant categories and subcategories, making it easy for both search engines and users to find what they are looking for.

Shoppable product images:

Invest in high-quality product images that showcase your products in the best possible light. Make sure to optimize these images for SEO by using relevant keywords in the alt text and fle names. This will not only improve your search rankings but also provide a visually appealing experience for your customers.

Compelling product descriptions:

Craft enticing product descriptions that not only highlight the key features but also incorporate relevant keywords. Use language that resonates with your target audience and speaks to their needs and desires. Remember, the goal is to not only optimize for search engines but also persuade potential customers to make a purchase.

Customer reviews and testimonials:

Displaying customer reviews and testimonials on your homepage is not only a great way to build trust but also provides valuable user-generated content. Positive reviews can enhance your search visibility and encourage potential buyers to trust your products and services.

Featured promotions and discounts:

Utilize banner sections on your homepage to showcase any ongoing promotions, discounts, or special ofers. This not only catches the attention of visitors but also provides a sense of urgency and encourages them to take action.

Clear and prominent call-to-action buttons:

Make it easy for your customers to take the desired action by incorporating clear and prominent call-to-action buttons. Whether it's adding a product to the cart, signing up for a newsletter, or contacting you, make sure these buttons stand out and guide users in the right direction.

Now that we have explored the key elements of an SEO-friendly shop homepage, let's dive into the effective use of banners and featured listings. These elements not only enhance the visual appeal of your homepage but also contribute to SEO optimization and highlight your best-selling products.

Strategically placing banners on your homepage allows you to draw attention to specific products, promotions, or seasonal ofers. Ensure that the banners are visually appealing and contain relevant keywords in the text or images. Consider using compelling phrases like Limited Time Ofer or Best Seller to create a sense of exclusivity and urgency.

Featured listings are another powerful tool to optimize your homepage for both SEO and customer engagement. Choose your best-selling products or new arrivals and showcase them prominently on your homepage. Optimize the product titles, descriptions, and images with relevant keywords to improve search rankings and entice customers to click and explore further.

Remember to regularly update your banners and featured listings to keep your homepage fresh and enticing for both search engines and customers. A well-optimized homepage not only attracts organic traffic but also helps in converting visitors into happy customers.

Here's a list of places where you can get your shop banners designed:

Canva: A user-friendly graphic design platform with a range of templates specifically for Etsy banners. It's great for sellers who want to DIY their designs with an easy-to-use interface.

Fiverr: A marketplace for freelance services where you can find graphic designers offering custom Etsy banner designs at various price points.

Etsy: There are many sellers on Etsy itself who specialize in creating custom graphics for Etsy shops, including banners.

Upwork: A platform for freelancers where you can hire professional graphic designers with experience in creating Etsy shop banners.

Freelancer.com: A freelance marketplace where you can post your Etsy banner design project and receive bids from graphic designers.

Utilizing shop sections effectively

Organizing your listings into shop sections can have numerous benefits for both you as a seller and your potential customers. Not only does it help create a more organized and visually appealing shop layout, but it also enhances the user experience by making it easier for shoppers to navigate through your products. Additionally, utilizing shop sections effectively can also positively impact your shop's performance in search engine optimization (SEO).

So, how can you make the most out of your shop sections? Here are a few tips and strategies to help you effectively utilize shop sections:

Create relevant and descriptive shop section names:

When naming your shop sections, it's important to choose names that accurately represent the types of products found within them. For example, instead of generic names like Miscellaneous or Other, opt for specific section names like Home Decor, Jewellery, or Handmade Clothing. This not only helps shoppers quickly identify the type of products they're looking for but also aligns with their search queries, improving your shop's visibility in search results.

Here are five examples of how you can categorize your listings for different types of Etsy shops:

Handmade Jewellery Shop:
Categories: Necklaces, Earrings, Bracelets, Rings, Custom Jewellery
Example: Separate sections for each type of jewellery, making it easier for customers to find specific items like 'Sterling Silver Necklaces' or 'Beaded Bracelets'.

Vintage Clothing Shop:
Categories: Vintage Dresses, Retro Tops, Antique Skirts, Vintage Coats, Accessories

Example: Organize clothing by type and era, such as '1960s Mini Skirts' or 'Vintage Leather Jackets'.

Art Supplies Store:
Categories: Paints & Mediums, Brushes & Tools, Canvases & Surfaces, Drawing Supplies, Art Kits
Example: Different sections for various art supplies, like 'Watercolour Paints' or 'Sketchbooks & Paper'.

Home Decor Shop:
Categories: Wall Art, Decorative Pillows, Lighting, Rugs & Carpets, Table Decor
Example: Group items based on their use in home decor, offering categories like 'Handmade Ceramic Vases' or 'Bohemian Throw Rugs'.

Natural Skincare Shop:
Categories: Facial Care, Body Care, Hair Care, Aromatherapy, Gift Sets
Example: Segregate products based on their application, such as 'Organic Face Serums' or 'Herbal Shampoos'.

Optimize shop section descriptions for SEO:

Writing compelling and keyword-rich shop section descriptions can greatly enhance your shop's SEO performance. Consider including relevant keywords and phrases that potential shoppers might use when searching for products in your shop. For instance, if your shop section is dedicated to handmade candles, you could include keywords like soy candles, hand-poured candles, or aromatherapy candles in the description. By doing so, you increase the likelihood of your shop section appearing in search results when customers are looking for those specific products.

Enhance the user experience through organization:

A well-structured shop with clear and logical sections not only makes it easier for shoppers to find what they're looking for but also encourages them to explore more products within your shop. Consider grouping similar items together within each section, allowing customers to browse through related products effortlessly. For example, if you sell handmade jewellery, you could create sections for necklaces, earrings, bracelets, and rings. This way, customers interested in necklaces can quickly navigate to that section and find a variety of necklace options.

Utilize cross-linking between shop sections:

Linking related shop sections to one another can further enhance the user experience and increase the chances of customers discovering more of your products. For instance, if you have a section dedicated to home decor, you could include a link or mention related sections like handmade candles or wall art within the description. This allows customers browsing the home decor section to easily explore other relevant sections within your shop, increasing engagement and potentially boosting sales.

By effectively utilizing shop sections and implementing these strategies, you can create a visually appealing and well-organized shop that not only improves the user experience but also boosts your shop's SEO performance. Remember to continually analyze and optimize your shop sections based on customer feedback and search analytics to ensure they remain relevant and engaging.

Chapter 13:
Advanced Techniques for Keyword Optimization

Long-tail keywords and their secret advantage

Ah, the power of long-tail keywords! As Etsy sellers, we're always on the lookout for ways to boost our products' visibility in search results. And that's where long-tail keywords come into play, my friends. They are the secret weapon that can help us target specific niches and attract the right kind of customers to our Etsy shops. Let's dive deeper into this magical world of long-tail keywords and uncover their hidden advantage.

So, what exactly are long-tail keywords? Unlike short, generic keywords like jewellery or art prints, long-tail keywords are more specific phrases that have lower search volume but higher intent. They are like the niche whispers in the vast Etsy

Long-tail keywords are more specific phrases that have lower search volume but higher intent.

marketplace, attracting customers who are looking for something unique and tailored to their needs.

One of the main advantages of incorporating long-tail keywords into your Etsy SEO strategy is the reduced competition. Think about it: if you're selling handmade boho-inspired earrings, targeting the keyword earrings might not work in your favor. That keyword is way too broad and highly competitive. Instead, using a long-tail keyword like handmade boho earrings for festivals will help you stand out and attract potential buyers who are specifically looking for what you have to ofer. It's like having a secret code that only your target audience understands!

Another secret advantage of long-tail keywords is the higher conversion rate they can bring to your Etsy shop. When someone uses a long-tail keyword in their search query, it indicates that they have a clear idea of what they want. They are ready to make a purchase and are actively seeking products that match their criteria. By incorporating these specific keywords into your listings, you increase the chances of attracting customers who are more likely to convert into buyers. It's like having a virtual shop assistant who knows exactly what your customers want and presents them with the perfect products.

I know, you're probably thinking, But how do I find these magical long-tail keywords? Fear not, my fellow Etsy sellers, for I have some tips to help you on your keyword research journey. Start by brainstorming relevant phrases that your target audience might use when searching for products like yours. Put yourself in their shoes and think about the specific features, occasions, or problem-solving aspects of your products. For example, if you sell handmade candles, think about keywords like soy lavender candles for relaxation or hand-poured candles for romantic evenings.

Once you have a list of potential long-tail keywords, it's time to do some research. Use keyword research tools like Google Keyword Planner or Etsy's own search bar to check the search volume and competition for each keyword. Look for keywords with moderate search volume and low competition to maximize your chances of ranking higher in Etsy's search results. And don't forget to keep an eye on your competitors' listings and see if you can find any untapped long-tail keywords that they might be missing out on.

Here are 10 examples of long-tail keywords, showing the transition from more general, broad keywords to specific, long-tail keywords:

Broad Keyword: Candles
Long-Tail Keyword: Handmade Soy Wax Scented Candles

Broad Keyword: Yoga Mats
Long-Tail Keyword: Eco-Friendly Non-Slip Yoga Mats for Hot Yoga

Broad Keyword: Men's Watches
Long-Tail Keyword: Men's Vintage Leather Strap Mechanical Watches

Broad Keyword: Wedding Dresses
Long-Tail Keyword: Bohemian Lace Long Sleeve Wedding Dresses

Broad Keyword: Coffee Mugs
Long-Tail Keyword: Personalized Ceramic Coffee Mugs with Quotes

Broad Keyword: Baby Blankets
Long-Tail Keyword: Organic Cotton Baby Blankets for Newborns

Broad Keyword: Wall Art
Long-Tail Keyword: Abstract Acrylic Large Wall Art for Living Room

Broad Keyword: Women's Boots
Long-Tail Keyword: Women's Waterproof Hiking Boots Lightweight

Broad Keyword: Vegan Skincare
Long-Tail Keyword: Vegan Anti-Aging Skincare Gift Set for Sensitive Skin

Broad Keyword: Handbags
Long-Tail Keyword: Handmade Vegan Leather Crossbody Handbags

And finally, my friends, it's time to sprinkle those carefully selected long-tail keywords into your Etsy listings. Make sure to incorporate them naturally and avoid keyword stuffing, as it can hurt your rankings. Use them in your titles, tags, and product descriptions to increase your chances of showing up in relevant search results.

Remember, the power of long-tail keywords lies in their ability to target specific niches and attract highly motivated customers. So embrace their secret advantage, put on your professional but fun Etsy seller hat, and let those long-tail keywords work their magic in boosting your shop's SEO!

Latent semantic indexing (LSI) in Etsy SEO

As an Etsy seller, you're always looking for ways to improve your search rankings and increase the visibility of your shop. One powerful technique you can use to achieve these goals is leveraging latent semantic indexing (LSI) keywords. LSI keywords are words or phrases that are closely related to your target keywords and can enhance the relevance of your listings in search results. In this section, we'll explore the significance of LSI in Etsy SEO and how you can make use of it to boost your shop's visibility.

So, what exactly is LSI? Latent semantic indexing is a technique used by search engines to analyze the relationships between terms and concepts. It allows search engines like Google to understand the context of a webpage by identifying related words and phrases. By incorporating LSI keywords into your listings, you can provide more context and improve the overall relevance of your content.

But why is LSI important in Etsy SEO? Well, it's simple. Etsy's search algorithm rewards listings that are highly relevant to a user's search query. By using LSI keywords, you can demonstrate to Etsy's algorithm that your listings are closely related to what the user is searching for. This can result in higher search rankings and increased visibility for your shop.

Now that you understand the significance of LSI in Etsy SEO, let's explore some strategies for incorporating LSI keywords into your listings. The first step is to conduct thorough keyword research. By using tools and techniques like Google's Keyword Planner, you can identify LSI keywords that are relevant to your niche and target audience.

Once you have a list of LSI keywords, you can start incorporating them into your listings. One effective strategy is to naturally include LSI keywords in your product titles, descriptions, and tags. For example, if you're selling handmade soap, you can include LSI keywords like natural ingredients, aromatherapy, or moisturizing to enhance the relevance of your listings.

Here are some examples of using Latent Semantic Indexing (LSI) keywords in different Etsy scenarios:

Handmade Jewellery Shop:

Primary Keyword: Handmade Earrings

LSI Keywords: Artisan crafted ear studs, bohemian style dangle earrings, unique silver hoop earrings, custom-made gold earrings, bespoke jewellery design

Custom T-Shirt Business:

Primary Keyword: Custom T-Shirts

LSI Keywords: Personalized tee designs, graphic print shirts, tailor-made slogan t-shirts, bespoke cotton tops, unique screen-printed apparel

Organic Skincare Boutique:

Primary Keyword: Organic Face Cream

LSI Keywords: Natural skincare products, eco-friendly moisturizer, botanical facial lotion, chemical-free skin cream, herbal skincare solutions

Vintage Home Decor Store:

Primary Keyword: Vintage Lamp

LSI Keywords: Antique lighting fixture, retro table lamp, mid-century floor lamp, classic decor light, old-fashioned desk lamp

Handcrafted Pottery Studio:

Primary Keyword: Ceramic Vase

LSI Keywords: Hand-thrown pottery, stoneware flower pot, clay art piece, bespoke pottery decoration, artisan-made urn

In each of these scenarios, the LSI keywords provide additional context and variations related to the primary keyword, helping to enhance the item's discoverability and relevance on Etsy's search platform. These keywords should be naturally incorporated into product titles, descriptions, and tags for optimal SEO performance.

Another strategy is to create variations of your target keywords and sprinkle them throughout your listings. For instance, if your target keyword is handmade jewellery, you can include variations such as artisan jewellery, unique jewellery, or custom jewellery. This not only adds more context to your listings but also helps you rank for a wider range of search queries.

Additionally, don't forget to analyze your competition. Look for successful Etsy sellers in your niche and see what LSI keywords they are using in their listings. This can give you insights into the most relevant and effective LSI keywords for your own shop.

By utilizing LSI keywords in your listings, you can greatly improve the keyword optimization of your shop and enhance your search rankings on Etsy. So, take the time to conduct thorough keyword research, incorporate LSI keywords naturally into your content, and keep an eye on your competition. With these strategies, you'll be well on your way to boosting the visibility of your shop and attracting more customers.

Balancing broad and niche keywords

When it comes to Etsy SEO optimization, striking a balance between broad and niche keywords is crucial. This will help you attract a wider audience while still targeting specific groups of potential customers. So, let's dive into some tips and tricks for finding that sweet spot between broad and niche keywords!

When optimizing your Etsy listings, it's important to use both broad and niche keywords strategically. Broad keywords are more general terms that have a higher search volume. They help you capture a wider audience and generate more organic traffic to your listings. On the other hand, niche keywords are more specific and tailored to a particular audience or product category. They allow you to target a specific group of potential customers and improve the relevancy of your listings for their search queries.

So how do you strike the right balance between these two types of keywords? Here are a few tips:

Research popular broad keywords related to your product category. These are the terms that are commonly used by people searching for similar products on Etsy. For example, if you sell handmade soap, broad keywords like natural soap, artisan soap, or vegan soap might be relevant. Incorporate these broad keywords into your titles, tags, and descriptions to capture a wider audience.

Identify niche keywords specific to your target audience. Think about the unique features, benefits, or characteristics of your products that may appeal to a particular group of customers. For instance, if you offer eco-friendly soap, niche keywords like zero waste soap, plastic-free soap, or sustainable soap could be relevant. Use these niche keywords strategically in your listings to attract customers who are specifically looking for eco-friendly options.

Analyze your competition. Take a look at other successful sellers in your niche and see what keywords they are using in their listings. This can give you valuable insights into which keywords are effective in your industry. However, avoid copying their keywords or content directly. Instead, use these insights to brainstorm new ideas and refine your own keywords.

Experiment and track your results. Etsy SEO optimization is an ongoing process, and what works for one seller may not work for another. So, don't be afraid to experiment with different combinations of broad and niche keywords. Monitor your traffic, conversions, and sales data to see which keywords are driving the most success for your shop. You can then adjust your keyword strategy accordingly.

Remember, finding the right balance between broad and niche keywords is all about understanding your target audience and catering to their specific needs and interests. By incorporating both types of keywords into your Etsy listings, you can expand your reach while still appealing to the customers who are most likely to buy from you. So, have fun exploring different keyword strategies and finding what works best for your shop!

Chapter 14: Content Marketing Strategies for Etsy Sellers

Creating blog content to support your Etsy SEO

As Etsy sellers, we all know the importance of staying on top of the latest SEO trends to increase the visibility of our shops. One effective strategy that often gets overlooked is content marketing through blogging. In this chapter, we will explore how creating blog content can support your Etsy SEO strategy and improve your shop's visibility and search rankings.

When it comes to creating blog content to support your Etsy SEO, there are a few key factors to keep in mind. Firstly, it's important to understand that

It's important to understand that search engines love fresh, relevant content.

search engines love fresh, relevant content. By regularly updating your blog with informative and engaging articles related to your products, you are signaling to search engines that your shop is active and relevant. This can lead to improved search rankings and increased visibility for your Etsy shop.

Secondly, blogging allows you to target long-tail keywords that may be difficult to incorporate into your product descriptions. Long-tail keywords are specific, niche phrases that potential customers may use when searching for products similar to yours. By creating blog content that focuses on these long-tail keywords, you have a better chance of ranking higher in search engine results pages and attracting targeted traffic to your shop.

Lastly, blogging provides an excellent opportunity to showcase your expertise and build trust with potential customers. By sharing valuable information and insights related to your products, you position yourself as a trusted authority in your niche. This can help to establish brand credibility and encourage repeat business and referrals.

If you are looking to create blog content to support your Etsy SEO, there are several platforms where you can start a blog. Here are some specific websites suitable for blogging:

WordPress.com: A popular and versatile blogging platform offering both free and paid options. It's user-friendly and offers a wide range of customization options.

Blogger (Blogspot): A free blogging service provided by Google. It's easy to use and integrates well with other Google services.

Wix: Known for its drag-and-drop website builder, Wix also offers blogging capabilities. It's ideal for those who want a visually appealing blog with minimal technical effort.

Squarespace: Offers sleek, professionally-designed templates that are particularly appealing for visually-focused blogs, such as those related to crafts and design.

Weebly: Another drag-and-drop website builder that makes it easy to create a blog. It's user-friendly and offers a range of design options.

Medium: A platform that focuses on the writing and content aspect, offering a clean and distraction-free interface. Great for those who want to focus solely on content without worrying about design elements.

Tumblr: A microblogging and social networking website that's particularly popular with creative and artistic communities. It allows for a mix of blogging and social media interaction.

Typepad: A reliable and customizable blogging service with built-in analytics. It's a paid service but offers robust features and support.

Your Own Website: Creating a blog section on your existing business website. This is a great way to drive traffic to your main site and keep your audience engaged with your brand.

Each platform has its own set of features and advantages, so it's worth exploring a few to see which aligns best with your needs and goals. Remember, consistent and high-quality blog content can significantly contribute to your SEO efforts and help drive traffic to your Etsy shop.

Expanding reach through content syndication

Have you ever wondered how to expand the reach of your Etsy shop and boost your SEO? Well, I'm here to tell you about the magical world of content syndication! It's a fantastic way to get your content in front of more eyes and drive more traffic to your shop.

So, what exactly is content syndication? It's the process of distributing your content, such as blog posts or articles, on other platforms or websites. This means that more people will have the opportunity to discover your content and, ultimately, your Etsy shop.

Let's dive into the first section of understanding content syndication for Etsy sellers, shall we? We'll explore how content syndication can expand the reach of your content and give your shop's SEO a boost.

Are you ready to take your Etsy shop to the next level? Well, identifying suitable content syndication platforms is a key step. These platforms not only align with your niche but also ofer SEO benefits for your Etsy shop.

But how do you find these platforms? Start by researching popular blogs, websites, or online magazines that cater to your target audience. For example, if you sell handmade jewellery, you might look for fashion or lifestyle blogs that accept syndicated content.

Here are a few websites and platforms where you can consider:

LinkedIn Articles: If your products are relevant to a professional audience or if you write about topics like entrepreneurship or small business strategies, publishing articles on LinkedIn can be beneficial.

Guest Post on Niche Blogs: Find blogs that align with your Etsy shop's niche. For instance, if you sell handmade jewellery, look for fashion or lifestyle blogs that accept guest posts or syndicated content.

CONTENT SYNDICATION
A fantastic way to get your content in front of more eyes and drive more traffic to your shop.

Content syndication is the process of distributing your content, such as blog posts or articles, on other platforms or websites.

Flipboard: A content aggregation platform where you can create your own 'Magazine' to share articles, including your own blog posts, thus increasing your reach.

Scoop.it: This content curation tool allows you to share your blog posts on specific topics, helping you reach an audience interested in your niche.

Reddit: You can share your content in relevant subreddits. However, make sure to adhere to each subreddit's rules and contribute to the community to avoid being seen as spammy.

Pinterest: Not just for image sharing, Pinterest allows you to link back to your blog content. It's especially effective for visually appealing products or DIY topics.

Buzzfeed Community: You can create posts under the Community section. If your content aligns with the Buzzfeed style and audience, this can be a good place to syndicate.

Email Newsletters: If you have a subscriber list, sharing your content through newsletters is a direct way to engage your audience.

When choosing platforms for content syndication, consider the relevance to your niche, the platform's audience, and how well it aligns with your brand and Etsy products. Remember to track the performance of your syndicated content to understand which platforms are most effective for your Etsy shop.

Once you've found some potential platforms, take a closer look at their domain authority,

audience engagement, and relevancy to your products. Remember, you want to choose platforms that have a strong SEO presence and attract the right kind of audience that would be interested in your Etsy shop.

Now, let's move on and optimize your syndicated content for SEO and Etsy promotion. This is where the real magic happens!

When it comes to optimizing your syndicated content for search visibility and Etsy promotion, there are a few key strategies to keep in mind.

First, make sure to include relevant keywords throughout your content. This will help search engines understand what your content is about and improve your chances of ranking higher in search results. For example, if you sell handmade soap, include keywords like natural soap or organic skincare in your content.

Next, consider incorporating strategic Etsy promotions within your syndicated content. This could be in the form of a call-to-action at the end of your article, encouraging readers to check out your Etsy shop or offering a special discount code for readers who make a purchase.

Lastly, don't forget to promote your syndicated content on your social media channels and in your Etsy shop's newsletters. This will help drive more traffic to your content and ultimately increase the visibility and sales of your Etsy shop.

Upselling and Cross-Selling on Etsy

Upselling and cross-selling are powerful strategies for Etsy sellers to increase revenue, improve customer satisfaction, and enhance the overall shopping experience. By implementing these techniques, you can encourage buyers to consider additional purchases that complement or upgrade their initial choice. This chapter delves into effective ways to upsell and cross-sell on Etsy, transforming single purchases into more valuable transactions.

Understanding Upselling and Cross-Selling

Upselling: This involves encouraging customers to purchase a more expensive item, upgrade, or add-on to enhance the product they are planning to buy. For instance, suggesting a larger size or a premium material option.

Cross-Selling: This strategy involves recommending products related to the item a customer is interested in or has already bought. For example, suggesting a matching pair of earrings for a necklace.

Implementing Upselling on Etsy

Product Listings: Use your product listings to showcase premium options. For instance, if you're selling handcrafted journals, you could highlight an option to add custom embossing for a little extra.

Product Photography: Include images showing upgraded versions or add-ons. Visual prompts can effectively entice buyers to consider higher-value options.

Detailed Descriptions: Use your product descriptions to explain the benefits of the upgraded versions or additional features.

Effective Cross-Selling Techniques

Bundled Listings: Create listings that bundle related products together at a slightly reduced total cost. For example, a skincare bundle including a cleanser, toner, and moisturizer.

Shop Sections and Tags: Utilize shop sections and tags strategically to group related products. This makes it easier for customers to find complementary items.

Personalized Recommendations: After a purchase, send a thank-you message and include recommendations for other items in your shop that the buyer might like.

Leveraging Etsy's Tools for Upselling and Cross-Selling

Variation Listings: Use Etsy's variation feature to offer options like sizes, colors, or other upgrades directly on the product page.

Etsy's Automated Emails: Take advantage of Etsy's marketing emails, which can include recommendations for items related to past purchases.

Best Practices for Upselling and Cross-Selling

Value Proposition: Always highlight the value or savings the customer will get from the upsell or cross-sell items.

Relevance: Ensure that the products you are upselling or cross-selling are relevant to the customer's original interest.

Customer Experience: Keep the customer experience at the forefront. Avoid aggressive sales tactics that might detract from it.

Feedback and Adjustment: Regularly review your upselling and cross-selling strategies based on customer feedback and sales data. Adjust your approach accordingly.

Upselling and cross-selling, when done correctly, can significantly boost your Etsy shop's revenue while also providing additional value to your customers. These strategies can help you build stronger relationships with your customers and increase the average order value. With thoughtful implementation and ongoing adjustment, you can effectively use upselling and cross-selling to grow your Etsy business.

Chapter 15:
Staying Ahead: Adapting to Etsy's Evolving SEO Algorithms

Keeping up with Etsy's algorithm updates

As an Etsy seller, staying updated with Etsy's algorithm changes is crucial to ensure the success and growth of your shop's SEO performance. Adapting and adjusting your SEO strategy based on these updates is essential for maintaining and improving your shop's visibility and sales.

But how do you keep up with these algorithm updates? Where can you find reliable sources to stay informed about the changes and SEO best practices? Let's explore some tips and tricks to help you stay on top of Etsy's algorithm updates.

Stay updated with Etsy's algorithm changes to ensure the success and growth of your shop.

1. Etsy Seller Handbook:

The Etsy Seller Handbook is an invaluable resource for sellers to stay updated on algorithm changes and SEO best practices. It provides detailed articles, guides, and tips to help you understand and navigate the ever-evolving world of Etsy SEO. Make sure to regularly check the handbook for updates and new insights.

https://www.etsy.com/seller-handbook

2. Official Etsy Forums:

The official Etsy Forums are a goldmine of information for sellers. The forums are filled with discussions, threads, and posts from experienced sellers and Etsy staff. Engaging in these discussions can provide you with first-hand knowledge and insights about algorithm changes, strategies, and success stories. Participating in forums can also network you with other sellers and help build a supportive community.

https://community.etsy.com/t5/Etsy-Forums/ct-p/forums

3. Social Media:

Follow Etsy's official social media accounts, such as Instagram, Facebook, and Twitter. These platforms often share important updates, algorithm changes, and tips to help sellers succeed on Etsy. Additionally, there are also many social media groups and communities solely dedicated to discussing Etsy SEO and algorithm updates. Join these groups to stay in the loop and connect with like-minded sellers.

Instagram: https://www.instagram.com/etsy
Facebook: https://www.facebook.com/Etsy
Pinterest: https://www.pinterest.com.au/etsy/
YouTube: https://www.youtube.com/user/etsy
Twitter: https://twitter.com/etsy

By staying informed and adapting your SEO strategy based on Etsy's algorithm updates, you can ensure continued success and growth for your Etsy shop. Remember, staying updated doesn't have to be boring; it can be a fun and exciting journey of learning and growth!

Future-proofing your SEO strategy

When it comes to future-proofing your SEO strategy on Etsy, taking a proactive approach is key. Instead of waiting for changes to happen and reacting to them, it's important to anticipate these changes and stay ahead of the curve. By embracing a proactive SEO approach, you can ensure that your Etsy shop is well-positioned for success in the ever-changing world of search engine optimization.

Monitoring industry trends and best practices is an essential part of staying proactive. Keeping a close eye on what's happening in your industry and understanding how it can impact your SEO strategy is crucial. For example, if there's a new algorithm update that favors certain types of content or keywords, you'll want to be aware of it and make any necessary adjustments to your listings or tags.

But how do you effectively monitor these trends and identify best practices? One way is to participate in online communities and forums where Etsy sellers share insights and experiences. These communities are often full of valuable information and can help you stay updated on the latest SEO strategies that are working for others.

Another useful resource is to follow influential bloggers or industry experts who regularly write about Etsy Selling, Etsy SEO and share helpful tips and techniques. Their expertise and experience can provide valuable insights and keep you informed about any changes happening in the SEO landscape.

Building a strong and resilient SEO foundation is another crucial aspect of future-proofing your strategy. This involves optimizing your shop's listings, tags, and descriptions with relevant keywords, ensuring they align with your target audience's search intent.

One way to do this is to conduct thorough keyword research to identify relevant keywords and phrases that your potential customers are using to search for products like yours. By incorporating these keywords

TAKE A PROACTIVE APPROACH
Monitor industry trends, best practices and stay proactive to future-proof your SEO strategy

into your listings, you increase the chances of your products being found by the right people.

In addition to keyword optimization, it's also important to optimize other elements of your shop, such as product images, titles, and descriptions. Each of these components contributes to the overall SEO performance of your shop and should be carefully crafted to attract both search engines and potential customers.

Lastly, don't forget about the importance of user experience. Search engines like Etsy value websites and listings that provide a positive user experience. This means having a fast loading website, easy navigation, and high-quality content. By focusing on these elements, you not only improve your shop's SEO but also create a pleasant experience for your customers.

Building a resilient brand on Etsy

In the competitive world of Etsy, establishing a strong and resilient brand is crucial for long-term success. This section will delve into practical strategies and tips to help Etsy sellers craft a memorable brand identity and maintain consistency across their shop. Let's break down the key elements for building a resilient brand on Etsy.

Define Your Brand Identity

Discover Your Unique Selling Proposition (USP): Identify what sets your products apart. Is it the unique design, the sustainability aspect, or perhaps the story behind each item? Your USP should be the cornerstone of your brand identity.

Create a Compelling Brand Story: Share your journey, inspirations, and the values that drive your business. A relatable and inspiring story can create a deep connection with your audience.

Design a Memorable Logo and Visuals: Your logo and visual aesthetics are often the first things customers notice. Ensure they reflect your brand's personality and appeal to your target audience.

Choose Your Color Scheme and Typography: Consistent use of colors and fonts helps in creating a cohesive look across your shop and marketing materials.

Consistency is Key

Uniform Shop Aesthetics: Ensure your product photos, banners, and overall shop layout consistently reflect your brand's aesthetic. This visual consistency helps customers recognize your brand easily.

Consistent Messaging Across Platforms: Whether it's your product descriptions, social media posts, or customer communication, maintain a uniform tone and style that aligns with your brand's personality.

Regularly Update Your Shop: Keep your shop fresh and engaging with regular updates, new listings, and seasonal offerings, all while maintaining your brand's essence.

Other Branding Tips for Etsy Sellers

Engage With Your Audience: Build a community around your brand by engaging with customers through Etsy conversations, social media, and email newsletters. Show appreciation for their support and gather feedback.

Leverage Packaging and Branding Materials: Use branded packaging, thank you notes, and business cards to make a lasting impression. These small touches can enhance the unboxing experience and encourage repeat purchases.

Tell Your Story Through Social Media: Utilize platforms like Instagram, Pinterest, and Facebook to showcase your products, share behind-the-scenes glimpses, and tell your brand's story in an engaging way.

Focus on Customer Experience: Exceptional customer service can set your brand apart. Prompt responses, addressing concerns effectively, and exceeding customer expectations can turn buyers into loyal fans.

By defining a strong brand identity, maintaining consistency, and implementing these branding tips, Etsy sellers can build a resilient brand that not only attracts customers but also fosters loyalty and trust. Remember, a resilient brand is not just about the products you sell; it's about the story you tell and the experiences you create.

Login to ChatGPT at: https://chat.openai.com/

ChatGPT Prompt for Creating Etsy Product Listings and Descriptions

Hello ChatGPT,

I would like your help in creating an Etsy listing for a product I'm selling. Please see the details below and craft a compelling product description that highlights its features and appeals to potential buyers.

Product Type: [Insert type of product, e.g., handmade necklace, organic skincare cream]

Materials Used: [Describe the materials used in the product, e.g., sterling silver, natural shea butter]

Product Features: [List key features of the product, e.g., waterproof, hypoallergenic]

Unique Selling Points: [Mention any unique aspects, e.g., custom design, locally sourced materials]

Keywords: [List relevant keywords for SEO, e.g., eco-friendly, vintage-inspired, gift for her]

Target Audience: [Describe your ideal customer, e.g., eco-conscious shoppers, vintage fashion enthusiasts]

Shop Name: [Your Etsy shop name]

Shop URL: [URL of your Etsy shop]

Any Specific Style/Tone: [Mention if you prefer a specific style or tone in the description, e.g., casual, professional, whimsical]

Additional Information: [Any other information you think might be helpful, like price range, backstory of the product, etc.]

Thank you for your assistance!

Note: Utilize ChatGPT for assistance in creating the initial draft and to streamline your workflow. After receiving the draft, make sure to carefully review and edit it according to your specific needs. Additionally, conduct any necessary research to ensure accuracy and relevance.

BONUS: CHATGPT PROMPT

Login to ChatGPT at: https://chat.openai.com/

ChatGPT Prompt for
Etsy SEO Keyword Suggestions

I am seeking assistance in identifying SEO keyword suggestions for my Etsy listing. Below are the details of my product. Please provide a list of relevant and effective keywords that can improve my product's visibility on Etsy.

Product Type: [Insert the type of product, e.g., handcrafted necklace, organic bath bomb]

Main Features: [Describe key features of your product, e.g., made with recycled materials, lavender scented]

Target Audience: [Define your ideal customer, e.g., environmentally conscious buyers, home spa enthusiasts]

Primary Use/Function: [Describe the primary use or function of the product, e.g., home decoration, stress relief]

Style/Theme: [Mention any specific style or theme, e.g., bohemian, minimalist, vintage]

Materials/Ingredients: [List the main materials or ingredients, e.g., sterling silver, essential oils]

Shop Category: [Your product's category, e.g., Jewellery, Beauty & Wellness]

Unique Selling Points: [Any unique aspects or selling points, e.g., hand-signed, limited edition]

Competitor Analysis: [Any known keywords used by competitors or industry trends]

Additional Notes: [Any other relevant information or specific considerations for the keywords, such as seasonal trends, cultural influences, etc.]

Based on this information, please provide a set of optimized keywords that could enhance the SEO of my Etsy listing.

Thank you for your help!

Login to ChatGPT at: https://chat.openai.com/

ChatGPT Prompt for Creating Social Media Posts and Hashtags

I'm looking to enhance my social media presence and would like your help in creating engaging posts and hashtags for my Etsy shop. Below are the details:

Etsy Shop Name: [Insert your Etsy shop name]

Shop URL: [Provide the URL of your Etsy shop]

Product Types: [Briefly describe the types of products you sell, e.g., handmade jewellery, organic skincare]

Target Audience: [Describe your ideal customer, e.g., fashion enthusiasts, eco-conscious buyers]

Shop's Unique Features: [Mention what makes your shop unique, e.g., custom designs, sustainable practices]

Themes/Events Coming Up: [Any upcoming themes or events you plan to promote, e.g., seasonal sales, new product launches]

Preferred Tone/Style: [The tone or style for the posts, e.g., friendly, informative, whimsical]

Special Offers or Promotions: [Any current offers or promotions to highlight, e.g., free shipping, discount codes]

Number of Posts Required: [Specify the number of social media posts you need, e.g., 10]

Preferred Social Media Platforms: [State the platforms these posts are intended for, e.g., Instagram, Facebook]

Any Specific Hashtags to Include: [List any specific hashtags you regularly use or want to include]

Additional Information: [Any other details you'd like to include, like specific images or product links]

Based on this information, could you please create [number] social media posts complete with engaging captions and relevant hashtags to help promote my Etsy shop?

THANK YOU

Thank you so much for investing your time in reading **Etsy SEO Secrets: Unlock The #1 Ranking On Search Results**. We hope that the strategies and insights shared in this book have empowered you to enhance your Etsy shop and achieve greater success.

LOVE YOUR FEEDBACK

Your feedback means the world to us and plays a crucial role in our journey.

We would be incredibly grateful if you could take a moment to leave a review on our Amazon page. Your review not only helps us improve but also assists other Etsy sellers in finding this resource that could make a significant difference in their entrepreneurial journey.

Your support and feedback are invaluable, and we can't wait to hear your thoughts.

Let's continue to grow and succeed together in the vibrant world of Etsy!

www.ingramcontent.com/pod-product-compliance
Lightning Source LLC
Chambersburg PA
CBHW071052290526
45795CB00004B/1444